The Intercessor's Guide

Raymond Chapman is Emeritus Professor of English in the University of London and former Deputy Chairman of the Prayer Book Society. He is a non-stipendiary priest in the Diocese of Southwark and is the author of numerous books, including *Leading Intercessions* (which has sold over 15,000 copies), *Hear Our Prayer, Stations of the Nativity, Stations of the Resurrection* and *Firmly I Believe: An Oxford Movement Reader.*

D1494452

Also by the same author and available from the Canterbury Press:

Leading Intercessions: Prayers for Sundays, Holy Days and Festivals and for Special Services, Years A, B and C

'It combines a masterful use of language in succinct expression, a profound understanding of liturgical prayer . . . and depth of devotion that will encourage in the way of prayer all who use these prayers.'
Tufton Review

'The prose is clear, dignified and appropriate for today.'
New Directions

'Beautifully written . . . [the] afterword "On Leading Intercessions" is very timely and should be read by all who embark on this ministry.'
Church Times

'Sensitive and pastoral.'
Church Observer

Hear Our Prayer: Gospel-based Intercessions for Sundays, Holy Days and Festivals, Years A, B and C

'This second neat little book of intercessions from Raymond Chapman is a useful addition to the bookshelf of anyone who regularly leads the prayers in public worship and doesn't always have time to create beautifully crafted original prayers of their own. The style is elegant and concise, and each set of prayers draws on the gospel for the corresponding Sunday, Principal Feast or Holy Day . . . For such a slim little book, there is a tremendous amount inside.'
Praxis News of Worship

Available from all good bookshops or visit our website:
www.canterburypress.co.uk

The Intercessor's Guide

*How to Plan, Write and Lead
Intercessionary Prayers*

Raymond Chapman

CANTERBURY
PRESS
Norwich

© Raymond Chapman 2007

First published in 2007 by the Canterbury Press Norwich
(a publishing imprint of Hymns Ancient & Modern Limited,
a registered charity)
13–17 Long Lane London EC1A 9PN

www.scm-canterburypress.co.uk

Second impression 2010

British Library Cataloguing in Publication data

A catalogue record for this book is available
from the British Library

ISBN 978-1-85311-791-6

Typeset by Regent Typesetting
Printed in the UK by CPI Bookmarque, Croydon, CR0 4TD

Contents

Introduction

There are many published books of prayers and advice about praying. The individual Christian who seeks help in personal devotions can draw on the riches of past centuries and the inspirations of the present time for adoration, thanksgiving, confession and personal supplication. The fact that there is little about the offering of intercessions in corporate worship is easily explained. Until very recently the accepted liturgies have included intercessions in set form, said by the officiant and with little scope for variation. One of the major changes in liturgical revision has been the opening of this privilege to lay members of the congregation. Many have been willing to assume this task and develop this skill – for it is a skill as well as an act of piety – and services have been enriched by the various insights and approaches brought into the regular pattern. There are books with suggested words for the intercessory prayers, but little attention to the wider view of what the intercessor needs to learn, in understanding what is being done and preparing to do it. This book is intended to help the faithful lay people – and perhaps the clergy too – who are taking responsibility for this important part of the service.

The first chapter considers the theology behind intercessory prayer in general. The second chapter explains how intercessions have been included in public worship from early times until the radical changes which have brought a new perspective and a wider opportunity. Those who want to go straight to particular matters may be disposed to pass over this section, but it is hoped that they will not: knowledge of what has gone before brings understanding of present opportunities. The following chapters take the intercessor through the process of planning and constructing the prayers, and standing up to deliver them. Things that can go wrong, even after the best intentions, are given a chapter to themselves. There is then some advice on personal preparation, both spiritual and mental. The last chapter gives examples of published forms of intercession with commentary on what they are meant to convey, and a selection of quotations from other writers.

The idea of this book came from Christine Smith at the Canterbury Press, to whom I already owe much gratitude for suggestions and support in preparing books of intercessions for use in the liturgy. May all who worship in our churches remember in their personal intercessions all those, known or unknown to them, who engage in this ministry.

Raymond Chapman

January 2007

1

Intercessory Prayer

To begin with, intercession is not the whole of prayer. Many people think of prayer in terms of asking God to give them what they want or believe they need, for help in difficulty or protection in danger. Such requests are part of the aspect of prayer which is called *supplication*. The word *pray* itself is derived from a word which means 'ask', or more strongly 'implore' or 'beseech'. When someone says, casually or with real meaning, 'Say a prayer for me', the wish is usually to be brought to the attention of God, and to receive his help or favour. Christians know that the duty and privilege of praying cannot be fulfilled by supplication alone. There should also be adoration of God for all that he is in himself, thanksgiving for material and spiritual blessings, confession of sins. The prayer of supplication includes *petition* for oneself and *intercession* for others. Petition is a personal encounter with God: intercession places ourselves as a channel between God and others. The word 'petitionary' is sometimes used to describe both types of prayer, and although we are going to concentrate on intercession, it is important to remember that all prayer needs to be held in the totality of faith and to be a part of the whole approach to God, in worship and daily living. Prayer acknowledges our entire dependence on God for all our needs and desires.

Although it is not the whole of prayer, intercession is not a 'low level' of prayer as some spiritual writers have tended to suggest, ranking it as inferior to meditation and contemplation. It is true that intercession needs to be verbalised and particularised. It does not call for an emptying of the mind to all that is external – although requests may be followed by periods of silent offering and reflection. The public and corporate intercession which will be our subject needs support from private prayer. The intercessor will be a person of prayer, and those who respond during the act of worship will take the spoken intercessions into their private prayers.

All prayer is formed and offered through our conception of the God to whom we pray. Any attempt at defining or describing God is necessarily inadequate. Even the words which we can partly understand – such as complete power, love, mercy, knowledge – seem to put limits on his infinitude by the very fact of naming them. The personal encounter of the individual with God may provide all we need to know and feel in our spiritual lives, but interceding for others requires some further clarifying, which perhaps is best done through negatives. What kind of God are we *not* addressing in our intercessions? Not the remote, impersonal God of Deism, sometimes likened to a clockmaker who winds up his creation and then lets it tick on by itself. Not a celestial problem-solver, a sort of giant computer to produce results if skilfully handled. Emphatically not a power to be invoked by the right formula, an Aladdin's lamp to bring aid whenever we say the right words. Any idea of magic, of human skill and knowledge imposing constraint on the spiritual, is opposed to true religion and has a nasty way of creeping in if we are not careful. Not a tyrant whose heart must be softened to change decisions already made. Not an indulgent nanny who will take over our lives and let us lazily avoid making any effort of our own.

Intercessory prayer in the Bible

The Old Testament has much to teach us about prayer, inter-cessory and of other kinds. Prayer is often linked with sacri-fice, a reminder of the fact that all worship is an offering to God in his majesty, not just an expression of human feelings. The Psalmist says,

> Let my prayer be counted as incense before you, and the lifting up of my hands as an evening sacrifice.
> Psalm 141.2

Early intercessory prayers are often simple and spontane-ous, like the prayer of Moses when Miriam is smitten with leprosy:

> 'O God, please heal her.'
> Numbers 12.13

Later prayers, especially those written in times of trouble and national suffering, may be longer and more formal. An example is this extract from the prayer in the Apocrypha concerned with the three faithful Jews thrown by Nebuchad-nezzar into the furnace:

> 'Do not put us to shame, but deal with us in your patience and in your abundant mercy. Deliver us in accordance with your marvellous works, and bring glory to your name, O Lord.'
> Prayer of Azariah 19–20

The God to whom the Israelites prayed was the saving and protecting God in whom they trusted. He was the God upon whom they could call directly, the One who brought forth the response of those who knew his name and his works. Christian prayer turns even more naturally and intimately to the God whom Jesus Christ taught us to call Father. It is a name which tells of one who demands no special preparations, who is always there, always ready to hear and respond. The Jewish scriptures also tell of a God who is always present and open to prayer, but the New Testament brings a greater intimacy. The incarnation opened a new way, prayer made through Jesus Christ as the divine channel for our human needs and desires. It also brought a great responsibility, leaving no place for self-ish or unconsidered prayer, for unworthy motives or any wish for the hurt of other people. Praying 'through Jesus Christ' at the end of each prayer, means trying to pray as Christ him-self would pray, asking only for the things patterned after his example. When we put our wishes into words before God, we open them to judgement.

If God is a loving father who knows the needs of his children, what is the purpose of intercessory prayer? The purpose is clear only if we understand that we are not trying to change the will of God or question his perfect love and wisdom, but to work to make that creative love more positive in the world. All prayer is a response to the calling of God:

> The Spirit helps us in our weakness; for we do not know how to pray as we ought, but that very Spirit intercedes with sighs too deep for words.
> Romans 8.26

A loving father expects his children to share his concern for other members of his family: not just to tell him their troubles and walk away, but to work together for the good of all. Sincere intercession implies willingness to help, offering ourselves to take part in the divine purpose. God does not need us, but he graciously desires our co-operation. If our communion with God is a reflection of Jesus' own intimate sonship, we shall bring to our heavenly Father our wills as well as our requests.

The first Christians knew this truth and obeyed it. The New Testament has many instances of earnest prayer for individuals and communities, at the time when the Church was developing and was threatened by contempt and persecution:

> While Peter was kept in prison, the church prayed fervently to God for him.
> Acts 12.5

St Paul continually prayed for his new converts as well as severely censuring them for their shortcomings:

> I do not cease to give thanks for you as I remember you in my prayers.
> Ephesians 1.16

and asked them to pray for him:

> I appeal to you, brothers and sisters, by our Lord Jesus Christ, and by the love of the Spirit, to join me in earnest prayer to God on my behalf.
> Romans 15.30

Other writers declare the duty of believers to pray for the needs of others:

> I urge that supplications, prayers, intercessions, and thanksgivings should be made for everyone.
> 1 Timothy 2.1

> The prayer of faith will save the sick, and the Lord will raise them up; and anyone who has committed sins will be forgiven . . . The prayer of the righteous is powerful and effective.
> James 5.15, 16

Our approach in prayer

The Lord's Prayer, the prayer which Jesus taught us, begins with adoration and acknowledgement of God's greatness, and then turns to supplications which are made in the plural form: prayers for sustenance, pardon, guidance, protection, are made not for *me* but for *us*. It may be said that Christian prayer, however personal, is always corporate. Even when we are alone, the Church, in heaven and on earth, is praying through us, and this is most strongly felt in intercessory prayer in a shared situation. Specific intercessions reach out to embrace all humanity, to connect with the total care of God for the particular and for the whole. Praying for people we know opens us, individually and in community, to be concerned for those unknown. Intercession desires the fulfilment of God's kingdom of righteousness for those who suffer from oppression, injustice, illness, deprivation. We do not go alone into the presence of God: he is our Father because he is the God of all people. Consequently, what we ask for ourselves or for others may sometimes have to be denied for the greater good of some we do not know.

If our belief in God carries this child-like trust in one to whom we can always turn spontaneously, there is nothing about which we cannot pray, if it is truly asked 'in the name of Jesus Christ'. Committed to following the love of Christ, we draw into intercessory prayer the needs of many. The great global problems are not too big, the smallest local concerns are not too small to be drawn into that love. Jesus said,

> 'Ask, and it will be given to you; search, and you will find; knock, and the door will be opened for you.'
> Matthew 7.7; Luke 11.9

shortly after saying,

'Your Father knows what you need before you ask him . . .
Your heavenly Father knows that you need all these things.'
Matthew 6.8, 32

This means that intercession is not begging for necessities
which might otherwise be withheld. What we offer is inspired
and made acceptable as part of God's plan for a world which
has been redeemed and reconciled through the Son. All that
we try to put into words is done within the mystery of faith,
knowing that our understanding is limited. Any way of speaking about the eternal truths will be inadequate, but it may be
said that we believe God wants us to ask, as a way of proving
our faith, and offering the whole of life to be drawn into closer
relationship with him. All our needs, our desires, hopes and
fears bring us closer to God when we express them in prayer.
We ask in the assurance of the Prayer Book collect that he is
always more ready to hear than we to pray, and that he gives
more than we desire or deserve.

But will our prayers be answered? Not necessarily in the
way we would have chosen, as we can learn from the prayers of
Jesus himself. In his Agony in Gethsemane he prayed,

'Abba, Father, for you all things are possible; remove this
cup from me; yet, not what I want, but what you want.'
Mark 14.36

A common human response is 'My prayer was answered', or
'My prayer was not answered', meaning 'I did or did not get what
I wanted.' But prayer in the name of Jesus Christ is always to
be offered together with the first petition in the Lord's Prayer,
'Thy will be done'. Prayers are 'answered' in different ways;
the old phrase, 'God says yes, no, or wait' remains true. To put
it another way, we are to rest content with what we have asked
in faith, not knowing the total result of our intercessions, not
judging by the limitation of a single visible change.

Trusting and accepting

Yet our human reason, itself the gift of God to his creatures, may prompt us to ask whether praying for something can actually alter the way things are or will be. We strive in faith to believe that formulating our desires helps to bring them closer to the will of God, and that should be enough, but we find that there are questions which will not go away. Can we expect God to interfere with the laws of nature for our or others' benefit, to make it rain during a drought or check an epidemic of disease? Such prayers have traditionally been offered, within Christianity and other faiths. Does the fact that we know more than our ancestors about the scientific laws of nature invalidate them?

There is no easy answer. We pray in ignorance and trust, offering the situation, acknowledging that natural laws and a regulated world are the work of God. He has not placed us in a random world where nothing is predictable and anything may change if we can bend his will. Trusting in the ultimate triumph for good of that divine will, we offer our needs so that they may be sanctified within it. Remembering that we are not concerned with the 'clockmaker' God of Deism, prayer is offered within the ongoing creativity which orders and sustains the world as it has been created. Prayer is powerful not because it causes God to make a sudden change in events but because it is offered with faith in his directing power. What is changed may not be the outward event, but the response of those either directly affected by it or lovingly concerned about it.

It is important not to find proof or disproof in the apparent 'results' of such intercessory prayer. There is plentiful evidence of miraculous healings and of impending disasters averted. These are cause for praise, not for a triumphalist demonstration to the world of what Christians can do. There is also plentiful evidence of long illness ending in death, of massive suffering from natural disasters. These are cause not for loss of hope and abandonment of prayer that does not seem to 'succeed', but for compassion and what help we can humanly give. At the heart of it all there is mystery, something beyond our comprehension. The gift of prayer is a way of showing our dependence, our concern for others, our desire to help. It is itself an act of guided will, which is an act of faith.

The Book of Common Prayer has several prayers for relief in such troubles as war and bad weather. Today they may seem naïve to some, but their strength is that they acknowledge both our absolute dependence on God, and our own weakness. We no longer believe that illness is likely to be the result of sin, but we cannot be too often reminded that we are living in a world redeemed yet where sin is still a reality. It may be little present comfort when things go wrong, but prayer offered with full sincerity means coming to God unconditionally and accepting our place in his world. Mind and heart become conformed to a different pattern when we say, 'Not what I will but what thou wilt.'

Prayer should not be regarded as a kind of additional emergency service, to be called upon only when all else fails. People with the most compassionate hearts can sometimes lurch from crisis to crisis, seeking to give help in specific troubles and forgetting the ordinary things which are going on around them. Relief of distress and help in the maintenance of regular living are equally work done in the name of God. Individuals and communities need to be upheld by prayer even when nothing has 'gone wrong'. Life should be joyful in a world redeemed, though that may be easier to say than to fulfil when there is even temporary friction or stress. Intercessory prayers sometimes seem to be emulating the public media in looking for the bad news.

It may be helpful to look at the prayer for the Church Militant in the Book of Common Prayer service of Holy Communion (see page 75). After asking that the offering of prayer will be acceptable, there is prayer for the Church, for Christian unity and for good government. Then the ongoing needs are addressed: the clergy to be faithful in ministry and personal life, the laity to be devout in worship and loving towards others. Then comes prayer for the various troubles and sorrows which afflict people, and memorial of the departed. Like the Christian faith which inspires it, the prayer embraces life in its wholeness. The suggested frameworks for prayer in more recent liturgies have similar concerns. Living in our present-day world makes us more aware than ever of the reality of global suffering which we try to address with compassion, while remembering that every aspect of life proclaims our dependence on God, our Sustainer as well as our Creator.

In formulating and offering intercession there is always the danger of despair, losing hope, no longer trying. There is another danger, perhaps more common, and certainly more insidious, of self-satisfaction. We have offered our intercessory prayers for many people and causes, we have done our duty, we have shown how much we care for the needs of others. We have posted the letters, and now it is for God to read them and respond; our part is done. It would be better to say that our part begins when the verbal prayers have been offered. There may be nothing that we can do in the immediate situation, or we may have been called to look at it with new eyes and work in a different way. There may be a global problem which is too vast for our minds to encompass but which has aroused in us deeper compassion and fresh insights into needs closer to us. Intercessions sincerely offered declare that intercessors, as individuals and as communities, are trying to live in accordance with the will of God.

If we tremble with awareness of our own inadequate words and imperfect understanding, remember that we have been called in our weakness, graciously allowed to share in the eternal work of redemption:

> God is greater than our hearts, and he knows everything.
> 1 John 3.20

He will accept in love what we offer sincerely and without self-importance.

Christ our Intercessor

There is another source of comfort, awesome and mysterious but supported by Scripture. Our Lord Jesus Christ is the great Intercessor for the world which he has redeemed by his saving death. Within a few decades of his resurrection and ascension, some of his followers were writing about this insight which had been granted to them. The Epistle to the Hebrews tells of Christ as the great High Priest, who by his own sacrifice on the cross did away with the sacrificial cult of the Temple and pleads for the human race through his eternal priesthood. The writer of the epistle assures us that

> He is able for all time to save those who approach God through him, since he always lives to make intercession for them.
> Hebrews 7.25

St Paul writes to the new Christians in Rome in similar terms:

Who is to condemn? It is Jesus Christ, who died, yes, who was raised, who is at the right hand of God, who indeed intercedes for us.

Romans 8.34

We are not to think of this great assurance in the crude and indeed heretical terms of the Son pleading to soften the heart of a stern and judgemental Father. Nor do we imagine some heavenly equivalent of our earthly intercessions, with the utterance of specific verbal requests. In this world, on the eve of his passion, he prayed through human lips for his disciples and for those whom they would bring to faith (John 17.9ff.) and had previously prayed that Peter's faith should not fail in time of temptation (Luke 22.32). Not seeking to understand the depth of the mystery, we believe that the sacrifice made by the Son of God in the days of his incarnation is eternally effective for the needs of the world. His ascension lifted our humanity into the heavenly glory and opened a new way for constant communion between the human and the divine. There is a reminder here of the Old Testament link between prayer and sacrifice, an image of the greater glory to come. Christ is not a suppliant but an advocate, a defender of all who stand accused by their own sin.

St Paul writes of Christ and also of the Holy Spirit as Intercessor:

The Spirit helps us in our weakness; for we do not know how to pray as we ought, but that very Spirit intercedes with sighs too deep for words. And God, who searches the heart, knows what is the mind of the Spirit, because the Spirit intercedes for the saints according to the will of God.

Romans 8.26–7

St John writes of Christ as Advocate:

If anyone does sin, we have an advocate with the Father, Jesus Christ the righteous; and he is the atoning sacrifice for our sins, and not for ours only but also for the sins of the whole world.
1 John 2.1

Christ is not offering justification through clever arguments like a lawyer in court, for he is the Righteous One, a title of the Messiah in the Old Testament. The word here for 'advocate', *parakletos*, is the same as Christ uses in his promise of the coming of the Holy Spirit (John 14.16, 26). The unity of the Holy Trinity is unbroken; the work of each Person is complete and inclusive. The heavenly intercession seems to take us to the heart of the mystery of God, three in one and one in three, and we dare examine it no further. The prayers we offer here are sanctified. They are not offerings to a God who is remote from our human condition. We pray to one who knows us not by divine omniscience alone, but by the experience of a human nature in a human body:

Still for us he intercedes;
His prevailing death he pleads;
Near himself prepares our place,
Harbinger of human race.
New English Hymnal, 130

It is the one Saviour of his Body, our Lord Jesus Christ, the Son of God, who both prays for us, and prays in us, and is prayed to by us. He prays for us, as our Priest: he prays in us, as our Head: he is prayed to by us, as our God.
St Augustine

13

2

Intercession in Public Worship

One of the most interesting and important developments in our churches during the second part of the twentieth century has been an expansion of the part played by lay members of the congregation in public worship. We have rediscovered the deeper meaning of the Church as the Body of Christ, with many members contributing in various ways to its integrity:

> For as in one body we have many members, and not all the members have the same function, so we, who are many, are one body in Christ, and individually we are members one of another.
> Romans 12.4–5

There has been a renewed understanding of the laity, not as a necessary but mostly silent majority in the Church but as the People of God: the word 'laity' derives from the Greek *laos*, 'people'. We have come to understand again that 'going into the Church' does not mean taking clerical orders, but being baptised and becoming a member of the eucharistic community. These truths have seldom if ever been openly denied, but they were for too long neglected.

Now at the Parish Communion it is likely that unscripted intercessions, usually within a familiar framework, will be offered, and that the intercessor will most often be a lay member of the congregation. We have rapidly come to accept and welcome this as a regular practice, but it is a recent practice in terms of Church history. To understand what has been happening in these changes and innovations, and to adapt to them most successfully, we should examine the liturgical tradition from which they have come. A balance between sound tradition and creative development is the making of worthy service. Since we are dealing with a new concept of what the liturgy may contain, we need to think about what we are doing, why we are doing it, and how it relates to our understanding of the Church today.

Intercessions in early liturgies

There is much that we do not know about the early Christian liturgies, but there is evidence of a Service of the Word on Sunday morning with lections, sermon and prayers. The Eucharist was celebrated on Sunday evening, followed by, or perhaps including, a fellowship meal. This meal was separated from the Eucharist at an early date and known as the *agape* or 'love-feast'; it gradually fell into disuse in the fourth century. Previously, probably as early as the second century, the Eucharist came to be celebrated in the morning and combined with the Service of the Word. Justin Martyr, writing around AD 140, records:

> We offer up prayers in common for ourselves, for the baptised person, and for all men.

As set liturgies developed, the 'Prayers of the faithful' which had come at the end of the *synaxis* or Service of the Word came to form part of the eucharistic prayer. In some early liturgies the intercessions were offered before the Prayer of Consecration, but as the idea of a 'moment of consecration' developed, they more often followed it. St Cyril of Jerusalem in 325 describes a Eucharist with prayer for the peace of the churches, for rulers, for the sick and afflicted and for the departed, following the *epiclesis*, the invocation of the Holy Spirit after the Prayer of Consecration. Prayer for the communicants, and the desire to associate the prayer with some special intention, led to development of this part of the prayer to include other petitions. St Cyril mentions belief in the special efficacy of prayers offered in the presence of the consecrated elements.

Local usage varied considerably in the early centuries, but there is clear evidence of prayers for the dead and for the living; prayers for the dead seem to have been the earliest individualised intercessions. While the early intercessory prayers at the *synaxis* were general – for travellers, penitents, catechumens and so on – intercessions at the Eucharist became more personal, using specific names. As the Roman rite came to be established in the Western Church, the intercessions, firmly placed in the Canon of the Mass after the Service of the Word was completed, returned to being made in more general terms, with set reference to certain saints of the Church.

The Book of Common Prayer

In England, the introduction of the First Book of Common Prayer in 1549 was the beginning of a slow return of the laity to active participation in the services of the Church. It was the first complete service book in English, although English versions of the Lord's Prayer, the Creed and the Ten Commandments had been printed in 1536, and an English Litany in 1544. This Litany, later incorporated into the Prayer Book, was composed with a particular intention of prayer at a time when England was at war with both France and Scotland. Its suffrages, based partly on previous litanies, are comprehensive, but general in reference, more like the prayers of the ancient *synaxis* than recent concepts of intercession. The prayers for guidance and for protection against various troubles are written in the optative mood – not the direct request to God but the expression of a pious hope: 'That it may please thee . . .' It is a form of address that would be usual in speaking to a monarch or person in great authority at that period in time. Confession of unworthiness and dependence precedes the intercessions and thus sets them within the pattern of holistic prayer.

The Prayer Book brought the services to the people, and the people to the services, in a way which had been lost for many centuries. The lay contribution was not large by later standards, but the congregation were exhorted to join in the forms of confession, in the Lord's Prayer, and in making various responses. The invitation to confession at Mattins and Evensong, made to 'as many as are here present', is not a redundant phrase but an assurance of corporate involvement.

However, the intercessory prayer in the service of Holy Communion was still to be said by the celebrant alone, the people simply responding at the end with 'Amen'. It kept its place in the canon of the Eucharist, after the Service of the Word ended with the sermon. In the 1549 book it came after the Sanctus – 'Holy, holy, holy, Lord God of hosts . . .' – beginning 'Let us pray for the whole state of Christ's Church' and continuing into the Prayer of Consecration without a break. In the 1552 book, which is the ancestor of the Book of Common Prayer as used today, it came after the offertory sentences and the preparation of the bread and wine. The phrase 'militant here in earth' was added to the introductory 'state of Christ's Church'. Prayers for the dead were replaced by thanks for their lives on earth and a petition for following their good example, and a prayer for the acceptance of 'alms' was added. This form, part of the revision of the book in a more Protestant direction, has been condemned by a twentieth-century critic of the Book of Common Prayer, writing in 1945:

> The intercessions in 1552 followed the protestant model in being a long monologue by the celebrant to which the people replied Amen; and not a corporate exercise in which all 'orders' play a co-operative part, as in the primitive rites.
> Gregory Dix, *The Shape of the Liturgy*

This may seem a little harsh in not acknowledging the break-through which Cranmer had made with the new services, but it anticipates the thinking which brought about radical liturgical change in the following fifty years.

The Elizabethan Prayer Book of 1559 made no substantial changes in this service except by combining the two sentences of administration into a continuous whole (1549, 'The Body of our Lord Jesus Christ . . .'; 1552, 'Take and eat this . . .'). When the Book of Common Prayer was revised in 1662, the prayer for the departed at the end of the Prayer for the Church Militant was restored, though in a modified form, and the word 'oblations' was added to 'alms' – leading to later disputes about its exact reference which need not concern us here.

The development of lay intercession

Although the Book of Common Prayer brought lay congregations into a stronger relationship with the worship being conducted by an ordained minister, it did not give them a much fuller part in the actual conduct of the services. In time, lay members would often read the lessons at Mattins and Evensong and the celebrant might add biddings for local as well as wider needs before the Prayer for the Church Militant, but there was no substantial change until the middle of the twentieth century. There was, however, a significant innovation in 1866 when the first Readers (then Lay Readers) were admitted. Their duties for some time were severely limited, but they gradually came to be given more authorisation, and are now an indispensable part of the Church's ministry.

The admission of other lay people to positions like intercessor and chalice assistant took longer in the making. In the twentieth century there was much discussion about the nature of the Eucharist and its importance in parish life. The dominance of Mattins as the principal morning service, with Holy Communion as a said early or late celebration, gradually gave way to the Parish Communion. Some churches had a mid-morning Sung Eucharist at which few if any of those outside the sanctuary communicated. The 'Parish and People' movement around the middle of the twentieth century worked to establish the centrality of the Eucharist, and its place as the offering of the People of God in which the whole congregation should regard itself as an essential part, but without advocating lay liturgical intercession. In 1959 one parish priest, Alfred Shands, had a layman read the Prayer for the Church Militant 'standing in the midst of the people . . . to make it part of the people's intercessions', but this seems to have been a rare, if not unique, instance. But a fresh understanding of intercessory prayer, which would eventually move in that direction, was in the nature of the movement. It was expressed by one of its leading writers.

Intercession . . . separated from Christian faith and the fellowship of Christians [is] treated as a psychological method for promoting human well-being.

Each individual member of a worshipping congregation should accept

> the meaning of Intercession as the realisation of the common life which he shares with [others] as a member of God's family . . . sharing the common burden of the humanity of which we form a part.
> A. G. Hebert, *Liturgy and Society*, 1935

It was not the Church of England alone which had failed to grasp the implications of drawing the laity more into the service. In those Free Churches which had a separated ordained ministry, the minister usually conducted the service, perhaps with a deacon or elder, but without further lay assistance. Indeed, for centuries the argument between the Church of England and the Free Churches was about set or extempore prayers in services, rather than who should say them. Nevertheless, the Free Churches took the position of their lay members more seriously and held in principle, if not always in liturgical practice, to the priesthood of all believers. Weekday prayer meetings brought lay people together to offer intercessory and other prayers. Family prayers, in both Anglican and Nonconformist households, also maintained the habit of shared prayer, sometimes entirely extempore and sometimes drawn from printed collections. Henry Thornton's *Family Prayers*, published in 1834 and often reprinted, was one of the most popular of the many available sources.

However, the Free Church contribution to the establishment of lay intercessions in services should be honoured. The Congregationalist minister Thomas Binney (1798–1874) believed that people should be

called vocally to utter some portion of the Church's *com-*

mon prayer, so . . . that they shall find that they positively *do* pray, as well as listening to another praying.

R. D. C. Jasper, ed., *The Renewal of Worship*, 1965 (italics in original)

This is the understanding which has gradually emerged with the use of lay intercession in services. The wise insight of a more recent Presbyterian minister leads towards the change which has come about in most of our churches, emphasising that private devotion should be closely related to public worship:

It is not something *done for him* by priest or minister, but something which *he is doing*, he and his fellow worshippers together; something which each of them, when they separate, will seek to continue individually as members of the Body of Christ.

R. D. Whitethorn, in R. D. C. Jasper, ed., *The Renewal of Worship*, 1965 (italics in original)

The *Sunday Service* book issued by the Methodist Church in 1974 put this Free Church principle into practice with the prefatory note:

At the Lord's Supper an ordained Minister, or a person with a dispensation for the purpose, shall preside. Laymen may be invited to share in the Preparation, the Ministry of the word, including the intercessions; and in the distribution of the bread and wine.

Liturgical revision

To return to the Church of England, the introduction of lay intercessions at the Eucharist came quietly and without any defining moment of a break with past usage. In fact the whole

21

process was distinctively Anglican: gradual, moderate, and pragmatic as new insights, needs and resources were matched. There was much prolonged and learned discussion over the succession of new services which were authorised, with particular attention to tracing eucharistic orders to their earliest recorded forms and seeking to adapt their pattern to the Church of the present day. The lay element came in mainly through rubrics in the orders of service themselves, each one making the lay offering of intercessions more possible, and at last normative. A series of quotations over many years of growth will show how we have come to the present position.

In 1927 and 1928 proposals for a revision and expansion of the 1662 Book of Common Prayer failed to get Parliamentary approval. The book was consequently not authorised for use in churches, but in practice many clergy adopted some of its provisions with tacit episcopal approval, or at least non-intervention. Much of it was incorporated into later authorised service books. It contained a rubric which might seem to have little bearing on lay intercessions, but which in fact pointed towards the direction in which the Church was going. It is very simple:

Subject to any directions which the Bishop may give, the Minister may, at his discretion, after the service of Morning or Evening Prayer or of any service contained in this Book, offer prayer in his own words.

Nothing about lay prayers, but permission for extempore prayer to supplement the set order of office and eucharistic services, and therefore able to be addressed to immediate and local concerns.

The Church of England Liturgical Commission issued a report in 1958, in which it made explicit what many had already understood about the position of lay members of the Church, partly through study of early liturgies and patristic writings:

> [A] layman is essentially a member of the Laos, the people of God . . . as a member of the people of God, the layman has his own proper responsibility in the offering of the Church's worship, in witness to the Gospel before the world, and in the government of the Church.
>
> *Prayer Book Revision in the Church of England*, p. 20

Still there is no suggestion of actually contributing to the service, but ideas are moving that way. Individual priests, especially those with specialist rather than parochial ministries, felt free to experiment further. About 1964 Gordon Phillips, then Anglican Chaplain to the University of London, produced an orthodox but radical liturgy for use at St George's, Bloomsbury. It was a simple duplicated booklet which he called *Reasonable Service* and it allowed one of the congregation to lead intercessions from the back of the church. Little noticed at the time outside the student community, and little remembered today, it initiated what would a few decades later become the norm.

In the 1960s a succession of booklets presented more official experimental orders of service in preparation for extensive liturgical revision. Through brief rubrics, they show the evolution of intercessions away from the clerical monopoly. Series 1 (1966) kept the general structure of the Book of Common Prayer, but with a stronger link with the First Prayer Book of 1549. It allowed for the Prayer of Intercession after the Offertory to be broken into sections, each with a congregational response, 'Hear us, we beseech thee'. In Series 2 (1967),

> The prayers of the Church may be offered by the Priest or by one of the other Ministers,

an instruction followed by a set form with spaces for special prayers. 'The Priest' is clearly the Celebrant – or the President, as the term which was coming into use. 'Ministers' is more open but seems to imply at least those robed and already in the service, the order for which begins, 'At the entry of the Ministers'. In Series 3 (1973) there is a leap forward:

> Intercessions and thanksgiving are offered by the President or by some other person.

A set order still follows but the introduction of specific subjects is made optional and there is a short concluding prayer for each section. The word 'lay' in this connection appears in a guide to the new services, issued by the Church Union in 1975, concerned largely with order and ceremonial and sacerdotal in its emphasis, but with a clear message. It envisages the 'Intercession or Prayer of the Faithful' with the celebrant saying the opening and closing sentences.

> The remainder of the prayer is suitably said by the deacon, by another priest, or by a lay person.
> *The Celebration of the Eucharist*, 1975

This publication had no official status, but work on the *Alternative Service Book* was already in progress. When it was introduced in 1980, the barrier had come down: 'Intercessions and thanksgivings are led by the president, or by others.' It may seem a small point of language, but 'others' is the culmination of a long development. Certain functions are still reserved to the ordained ministry, but there are parts of the eucharistic service in which the participation of clergy and laity is equally valid. Further freedom was granted in the form and content of the intercessions, in words which almost collapse under the weight of the wish to be comprehensive: 'The form below or one of those in section 81, or other suitable words, may be offered.' When the even greater flexibility and multiple choices of *Common Worship* became available in 2000, it was no longer necessary to specify who was authorised to pray. The heading 'Prayers of Intercession' is followed by the simple passive statement: 'One of the forms on pages 281–289 or other suitable words may be used.' The now familiar fivefold division of subjects of intercession for particular purposes is suggested and 'may be used'.

Now both clergy and laity were empowered to take on the responsible task of intercessions at the Eucharist with full authority and in good heart.

3

Planning Intercessions

The Liturgy of the Word

In reviewing the history of the Christian liturgy, we have seen how the early *synaxis* or Ministry of the Word, derived from Jewish synagogue worship, was brought into the Eucharist. Most liturgies over the centuries have shown a similar pattern, moving from the gathering of the people and introduction to the service, the collect for the day, Bible readings, a sermon or homily for instruction, corporate confession of faith in the Creed, with the offertory marking the beginning of the celebration of the sacrament. The most notable variant has been the position of the intercessions. The Book of Common Prayer puts the long prayer of intercession after the offertory, beginning with a petition for acceptance of the 'alms and oblations', thus continuing the medieval usage of such prayers being made by the celebrant.

The more recent liturgies which are in use today, together with the Book of Common Prayer, have moved the interces-sions to earlier in the service and opened them to people other than the Celebrant or President. The eucharistic order in *Common Worship* recognises the Gathering, with preparation, confession and absolution, the Gloria and collect of the day. The Liturgy of the Word follows with one or two scriptural readings leading to the Gospel, the Sermon, Creed, and then the intercessions, with the Peace leading into the Liturgy of the Sacrament. The modern Roman Mass follows the same pattern, which is also similar to what is done in many of the Free Churches.

In this structure, the intercessions come as the culmination of a time for preparation and learning before the greatest offering of the Church is made yet again, following the commandment of Christ. Now that they are given this special place, it is important to see them not as just a series of petitions to God, set apart from the celebration of the sacrament which is to follow. There should be no suggestion of 'now is the time for a few requests before we move on'. Intercession is made in the total context of the act of worship, from the greeting to the final blessing and dismissal. The intercessions should draw together what has just been heard, taught and confessed, leading the whole congregation towards the shared communion. They should strengthen the relationship of the gathered people with God and with those for whom we are praying, drawing the divine and the human into one affirmation of faith.

The intercessor therefore has a corporate role. This is not to be a personal performance, but an individual act which has a kind of hiddenness, as the individuality of the President is hidden in the authority of being the priest at the altar. Yet in both priest and lay minister, something of the individuality remains. Each will have the personal stamp, the distinctive voice and presence which make the action repeated but ever fresh. One is standing for a moment alone, yet intimately related to all who are present and turning them towards God. This may sound rather intimidating set out in words, but the grace of God accepts our imperfections and turns them to holiness. Intercessors will try to relate their prayers to the great prayers of the Church, while keeping individual spontaneity, the diversity of gifts which is part of our glory in God's creation.

As the intercessory prayers form the conclusion of the Ministry of the Word, it is desirable to make some connection with the readings for the day. Some intercessors may prefer to base their prayers on the Gospel alone. The Revised Common Lectionary works through the three Synoptic Gospels (Matthew, Mark and Luke) in turn through a year beginning in Advent, and this has brought a welcome continuity of style and approach to the eucharistic readings. Intercessions may also take account of the other readings; the use of a passage from the Old Testament has strengthened the relationship with tradition. It is not necessary always to make overt references, and the connection should certainly not cause any anxiety or constraint in preparation. The variety and richness of the biblical readings will give plenty of scope without limiting the freedom of local needs and specific petitions. There are no Sunday 'themes' in the current lectionaries as there were for the *Alternative Service Book*. Some days and seasons in the Church's year naturally have their own distinctive directions of thought and prayer. Other Sundays may suggest a framework for what is to be offered through intercession.

It is worth remembering that although intercessions today most often form part of a eucharistic service, they may equally well be included, with many of the same considerations, in other acts of worship such as the popular Family Service.

Subject groups

It has become customary to divide the intercessions into groups directed towards specific concerns. Here again, the aim is for guidance, not for constraint, and custom need not be slavishly followed. It is generally helpful to the intercessor and to the congregation if there is a pattern to avoid rambling and unconnected prayers, and the fivefold division gives a logical sequence. Clear sections also allow for pauses with congregational response:

Lord in your mercy – Hear our prayer.
Lord, hear us – Lord, graciously hear us.

A greater freedom for intercessory prayers has developed through recent orders of service. The *Alternative Service Book* had clearly defined sections but no headings. In *Common Worship* the topics are simply listed, with the advice, 'The prayers usually include these concerns and may follow this sequence'; more specific and textual alternatives are also given. The *Alternative Service Book* provided short prayers to end each division. This is not done in *Common Worship*, but such prayers are provided in many books of published inter-cessions. In considering the fivefold division which has come to be commonly used, the topics may be discussed under the headings given in *Common Worship*. It should be emphasised again that these can be helpful guides in the organisation of public prayers but should neither limit the spontaneity of the intercessor nor themselves create a rigid liturgical order.

The Church of Christ: his creation and continuing Body on earth; bishop and clergy; parish; other Christians

As our intercessions are being offered within an act of public worship, we pray first for the Church as the Body of Christ on earth and for Christ's people in their lives of service. We know well enough, but it is easy to forget, that the Church does not mean the building in which we are present for the moment, or our own denomination. Wherever Christians gather in prayer, and above all in the Eucharist, they are praying with the whole Church. In a great cathedral, in a small suburban or village church, in a solitary sickroom, human intercession is joined with the perpetual worship of heaven.

Because our understanding is best served through the particular and familiar, it is good to pray for the Church leaders whom we know, at least by name. Prayer for the diocesan bishop has been customary since the early days of liturgy. Others who bear local responsibilities, and the clergy of the parish in which we worship, need support in prayer. Happily, we have come to a point in time when we pray without strain or condescension for Christians of other church confessions, remembering especially those in local churches, where there may be an ecumenical covenant or council of churches. There may be particular needs, such as the search for a new incumbent or minister, or necessary restoration work on church property. As Christianity grows in other parts of the world, notably in Africa, we can pray for churches overseas, for missionaries and for the faith expressed through customs and traditions different from our own.

If these, and similar suggestions under other headings, seem to be too extensive and to be in danger of resembling a shopping list, remember that not all will be needed at one time – and that there may be many others in any local situation. If the restoration fund and the mission field seem disproportionate in relation to each other, it reminds us that nothing is too small or too big to be offered in prayer. God is greater than our hearts, and is not too busy managing the universe to care for the fall of a sparrow – or could we venture to say, of a tile from the church roof.

Creation, human society, the Sovereign and those in authority

The *Alternative Service Book* suggested that the intercessions should begin with

> Let us pray for the Church and for the world, and let us thank God for his goodness.

It is a good aspiration, but it could have suggested to some a severance between Church and world. They are different but inextricably related. The 'Church Militant here in earth' of the Prayer Book, the Church which is Christ's body in this world, is composed of living believers in their present situation and given form and structure in ways which must often resemble those of the society around them.

This is the world which God created and Christ came to save. We need to be fully aware of the world, of its reality and importance. God's perfect creation is fallen and yet redeemed. People were made to live and work together, to honour fellowship as well as the individuality which makes each one of us unique in the divine purpose. We pray for all human needs and that the lives of people and nations may lead towards the coming of God's kingdom on earth. The world itself has become smaller with enhanced travel and communications, so that some speak of the 'global village'. There is a new sense of shared responsibility, which our ancestors could not know, for the very preservation of the planet itself. It has never been more necessary to pray for those who exercise power, not only political but economic and financial.

Our duty to the Church and for the world should never be kept in separate compartments. We need to recognise the material preoccupations of secular society and to pray lovingly and without condescension for those who endure the pressures of life without faith. Christians who know that their true home is in heaven are to be more, not less, concerned for the world in which they live. When Jesus said,

'I have come that they might have life and might have it more abundantly.'
John 10.10

he gave a promise and an instruction for life here as well as hereafter.

The local community

Next we move to the concerns that are nearer to us: families, friends, neighbours, those with whom we work. Even in our 'global village', we cannot avoid our strongest feelings being for the familiar and immediate. Nor should we feel guilty about this, for the greater loyalties in life nearly always grow from the lesser. Prayers for the wider world are often necessarily general, but here we can make our requests known more specifically, and in so doing the imagination may open greater sympathy for those who are far off and unknown. The phrase 'families and friends' may seem in danger of becoming tired and hackneyed by repetition, but it expresses something very dear to all of us. It is through experiencing human love, with all its limitations, that we come nearest to understanding the infinite love of God. Everyone in the congregation will have a particular application for those closest to them. We may pray also for those whom we shall meet at work or in leisure during the coming week.

We pray for all who live in the area that forms our local community, whether it is large or small. Here too worshippers will want to bring their personal lives before God and relate them to their social dimension. Prayer for what is local should be informed prayer. Authority and influence, sometimes difficult to comprehend in the great affairs of the world, are exercised also in local government and business. Those who administer and teach in our schools have responsibilities and privileges in decisions which affect many families. Those who work in social services often endure stress and frustration in doing the work of relief which is their chosen vocation. There are residential homes for old people in many parishes which need the support of prayer for those who live in them and those who run them, and for clergy and pastoral workers who visit them.

Those who suffer

Some people perhaps see prayers for the relief of suffering as the main purpose of intercession. It has already been suggested that ordinary daily life is also to be commended to God; and that the goodness in so much routine living is not to be lost in thinking only of what is wrong. Yet suffering is a reality and draws us to prayer. We pray for those who are in sickness, whether temporary or chronic, and for the work of all engaged in the work of healing and in caring for the sick. We remember too those who are in the grip of addiction to drink, drugs or gambling. It is too easy simply to dismiss them as having chosen their own way of life, and lose compassion for the compulsions which can overcome the individual human desire for better things.

These prayers can draw together the more general prayers for the wider world and the closer concern for local affairs. We can pray by name for the sick who are known to us, and we can pray also for those we shall never see. Our praying for particular people can concentrate the love which we hope will spread to those we do not know. We pray for those who suffer from continual hunger and unrelieved disease, for those who suffer persecution for their beliefs; for refugees, for those made homeless by war or natural disasters. We know so much more about these things than people did in the past. There is probably not more sadness and suffering in the world than there has ever been, but the present age has brought problems of its own and has also made us more aware of them. A few generations ago, most people knew of little beyond their own locality, but now the media bring us daily images of distress. The two dangers that result are either despair and a feeling that nothing can be done, or familiarity which gradually blunts compassion. Intercessory prayer can be a path of hope between the two.

The compassion of God reaches out to all but is too often blocked by human sin and indifference. Those who suffer are particularly dear to him, and as we pray for them we are offering our own sympathy and desire to help those, known or unknown to us, who are afflicted.

The Communion of saints

Prayers for the dead may be more controversial than prayers for the living. Some Christians believe that death brings final judgement and that the souls of the departed are beyond our human prayers. It is a position which must be respected, but most believe that the great chain of perpetual prayer links the Church Militant on earth with the Church Triumphant in heaven. The early liturgies included prayers for the dead, at first for martyrs and confessors but soon also for other faithful departed. Some medieval abuses which suggested a mechanistic and even commercial view of gaining relief for souls in purgatory brought a reaction which banned such prayers from worship in churches of the Reformation. This crude temporal notion of purgatory is in the past, and need no longer inhibit the offering of prayer by the living for the dead, a token of continuing concern and love joined with the eternal intercession of Christ.

Such prayers sanctify a natural human instinct of remembrance, still seen in our more secular society when flowers and messages are left at the site of a sudden death. Anniversaries of death are often remembered by a visit to the grave, and it is an ancient custom, worthily continued in many churches, to pray for those whose anniversaries of death have come round as well as for those who have recently died. The day of All Souls, 2 November, is a commemoration of the faithful departed, as the preceding day, All Saints, celebrates those known as great exemplars of the faith. It is appropriate to pray for the recently bereaved together with the departed, or to include them among those who suffer.

As we offer our prayers for the dead we recall our own mortality and affirm our faith in the resurrection to eternal life, and in the fellowship of all Christians, living and departed. The prayer for a holy death is not a very popular devotion today, when death itself has become almost a taboo subject and serious mention of it dismissed as morbid. The Christian should not think it so, and will quietly pray for this grace whenever there are intercessions for the dead.

All these things seem to make up a formidable list but, like examination questions, not all are to be attempted at one time. We still have to think about organising intercessory prayers with regard to length and particular detail. Division of human concerns into this fivefold pattern, or any other, is a needful concession to help our finite minds. Above it all stands the great truth that God is immanent as well as transcendent:

fully present in every aspect and detail of his creation as well as being above and beyond it. Our prayers express a deep relationship, moving our wills towards God, not his towards us. Let us also remember that through the incarnation of our Lord Jesus we can think of divinity as holding direct experience of life in this world, as well as the divine omniscience from which nothing is hidden. It is a strange and wonderful thought, which comes to the heart of Christian faith.

4

Organisation and Delivery

Religion and language

We need to use words in response to the silent calling of God within us. It is through language that we express our deepest concerns, our joys and desires in human relationships. It is through language that we set them out before God. Language is a divine gift, an organised system which enables us to communicate and thus to co-operate with others, to shape our personal thoughts, to create beauty. All these things are part of our humanity, and are relevant to our prayers, individual or corporate.

The novelist E. M. Forster wrote scornfully of 'poor little talkative Christianity', contrasting it with what he saw as more contemplative eastern religions. It is true that we are too often neglectful of silence, more ready to say, 'Hear, Lord, for thy servant speaketh' than to respond with Samuel, 'Speak, Lord, for thy servant heareth'. Silent waiting upon God has a vital place in personal prayers, and is important in public worship, although we have given it little attention in our modern liturgies. But what Forster did not understand is that Christians have a personal God, not a set of deities or an abstract sense of the Other but a relationship which graciously permits access from our humanity with all its limitations. It is an understanding which we share with the other Abrahamic faiths, Judaism and Islam, but for the Christian the relationship is confirmed and focused through the divine humanity of Jesus Christ.

Our intercessions must be offered through the words which we are accustomed to use and our hearers to understand. Yet there is a difference between everyday speech and the language of worship. The language of religion is in some ways necessarily 'odd'; it uses the words and grammar of our daily communication, but it is dealing with things which are not part of ordinary life. It must be related to common communication if religion is a real and most important part of our lives, but we shall inevitably be using words which are special and different. The very mention of God, used carelessly by so many people, opens a dimension beyond the concerns of daily living.

We cannot speak of our faith without using words like 'sin' – another word much misused and not taken seriously – 'salvation', 'incarnation', 'resurrection' and many others. While it is the task of the Church through all its members to try to make the ideas which these words represent understood in a secular society, we cannot get very far without them. To use them in an intelligible context is not such a formidable task as it may appear: the English language today is creating new words as never before and people have no difficulty in acquiring new vocabularies to meet their special needs. Computers have produced a whole vocabulary of their own, including both new coinages and a new definition of words like 'monitor' and 'mouse'. Every specialist interest has its own area of language shared by its members.

We do in fact change our language, usually without conscious effort, according to situation and relationship. We do not speak in exactly the same way to family and close friends, to strangers, in public address; and there is usually some difference between spoken and written communication.

These adaptations are known as a change of language *register*. Is there a special register for worship? For many centuries the religious register of English has been the language of the Book of Common Prayer and the Authorised or King James Version of the Bible. The style adopted at the time of their making took a firm hold on the religious response of English-speaking people, in Britain and in many parts of the world. Tudor English, adapted and elevated for worship, gave dignity and reverence which endured through changes and controversies. Today many still go instinctively to this register for prayer, and many who do not regularly engage in worship would think of it as somehow the 'proper' way of praying.

Language and liturgy

Whatever style we prefer in our private prayers, the inter-cessions in church are likely to be offered in services using modern language. *Common Worship* provides traditional language liturgies for both Order One and Order Two – the latter being in almost all respects the service of Holy Communion in the Book of Common Prayer. In a traditional language service, the traditional register is appropriate. But has a complete religious register for present-day English been developed? There is a discernible type of language which has passed through twentieth-century revisions to give a certain style which appears in *Common Worship* and in service books used by other churches. It is not so consistent or well marked as the traditional form, and it may be that such uniformity is not possible in present-day English. The language is continu-ally changing, especially with the introduction of new words and idioms, and our society does not look naturally for a register to express mystery and reverence as people did in the past. So there is both a challenge and an opportunity, not only for the makers of liturgy but for all who take part in public worship.

The intercessor should try to work in the style of the service – whether traditional or modern – without losing contact with the rest of the liturgy, yet also without losing the personal approach which gives diversity within the uniformity of shared worship.

It is desirable to study carefully the words of the service within which intercessions are to be framed. Total uniformity is neither possible nor desirable, but an obvious change of style is in danger of wrenching the intercessory period out of the preceding Ministry of the Word which is reaching its culmination. Intercessions should be a bridge between what has gone and what is to follow, not a gap which has to be crossed before continuity begins again.

Working within a certain style while keeping the stamp of the individual is not easy, but it is worth persevering. Artificial piety with a striving after linguistic effect is painful and easily detected. The goal is for dignity without stereotyping, reverence blended with intimate assurance. Elegance of language is not a short cut to God; but care with language helps to make a worthy offering and to keep the attention of the congregation. It is sometimes piously said that 'only the best is good enough for God'. Our human best will always fall far short of the divine perfection, but that should not make us content with offering less than the best we can achieve. Probably no one will ever produce the modern equivalent of Cranmer's work on the Book of Common Prayer. Changes in the language itself, and in shared attitudes to language, make such an attempt improbable and perhaps undesirable. But his desire to allow people to worship in language which they could understand, but which was worthy of its high intention, has been in the minds of modern writers of liturgy and can be felt by any who take a part in public worship.

The individual habit and preference of the intercessor has to be recognised, honoured, and at the same time modified where necessary. Many older people, and a good number of young as well, fall naturally into the traditional or Prayer Book style for their devotions. Others whose experience has been only of more recent service books may not have given much thought to the language in which they are written, and need to see it as a distinct register although not so well defined as the old. There has been much controversy about the proper style for worship; different opinions are to be respected but not made into barriers excluding either form of language. The Church, and perhaps particularly the Church of England, has been likened to the man of whom Jesus spoke as bringing forth from his treasure things new and old (Matthew 13.52). Traditional prayers can be adapted for a modern language service, or more recent prayers conformed to the traditional style.

This is a process which needs careful preparation, writing out and checking the consistent use of pronouns and verb forms. Some can make the transition extempore, as there are some who can sight-read music, but most of us prefer not to take any chances. A mixing of styles loses the qualities of both; an uneasy fluctuation between 'thou' and 'you', between 'have' and 'hast', is distracting to the congregation and could divert attention from the content of the intercessions to trying to guess when the next deviation will come. It may be useful to look at the two versions of the Collects in *Common Worship*, in modern and traditional language, as an example of adaptation. They include Prayer Book Collects revised in accordance with a modern language service, and some new ones rendered in words which do not jar in a traditional language service.

These intercessions, like all prayers, are offered to God,

whether addressed as 'thou' or 'you'. Unlike private prayers, they are made on behalf of, and in the presence of, a worshipping congregation. It is reasonable therefore either to make direct address to God with a beginning like

Almighty God, guard and direct the Church

or to speak in the form of a statement expressing shared desires:

We pray that the Church may be guarded and directed.

It is best to keep the same style of address through the whole set of intercessions. Whatever form is used, it is important for the special role of the intercessor to be kept in mind. Like the President, the intercessor stands in a Godward position, representing the whole congregation and presenting them to God. At the same time, he or she is the human representative of God to his people, the channel through which grace flows to the gathered people. We trust that God will graciously hear us through any muddle or obscurity of language, but our fellow humans who are praying with us need clarity.

Personal prayer may sometimes bring the privilege of being lifted above awareness of our immediate surroundings and situation to quiet contemplation, but such a state of rapture would not be useful during a service. The congregation needs to understand what is being said, and also to know how to play their part. Liturgical intercessions are not a monologue. Nor are they a game in which everyone tries to guess the intentions of the leader. The time and manner of united response should be made clear at the outset, for example:

Lord, in your mercy – Hear our prayer.

Lord hear us – Lord, graciously hear us.

or other versicles and responses known to all and sustained through the whole prayer.

While the language used should respect the worship of the universal Church, it should also respect local tradition. If the church in question habitually refers to 'the Holy Table', it would be insensitive to speak of 'the Altar', whatever one's personal preference. Some congregations may like a generous invocation of saints at the end, others may abhor it. There is usually no difficulty when regular members of a congregation habitually take a turn as intercessors, but clergy and laity who do occasional duty in different places need to get an idea of what is expected. Differences of churchmanship, happily no longer so divisive as they were in the past, can provide a firm platform where they are shared, but may become a stumbling block if they are insisted upon in a different tradition.

As has been said, a certain amount of special vocabulary cannot be avoided in liturgy and theological language, but let the intercessor who has had some theological training beware of using learned words. It is a splendid thing that more people other than clergy and trained Readers are now taking courses in Christian doctrine and history. The precision of some established words which help the student may not convey meaning to all. It is better to pray that we in our Church will always acknowledge the full humanity of Christ than to pray that we may be kept free from Docetism. We can keep before us the old cartoon in *Punch* of a preacher addressing a rural congregation and saying to them, 'Ah, I know what you are all thinking – Sabellianism' (an early heresy about the Holy Trinity).

Composing the intercessions

The question of whether to write out a full script or to use notes has to be decided by all who speak in public, and the answer is not the same in all cases. Since the period for intercessions is short, there is much to be said for having the complete words: it gives confidence and avoids awkward pauses and uncertainties. This is usually the best way for those who are new to this kind of participation in church worship. With a little experience, prayers put together under certain prepared headings will come more easily. The disadvantage of a full script is that reading often sounds very plainly like reading. This casts no shadow on the sincerity of what is being said, but it may appear less dynamic and less likely to involve the whole attention and participation of the congregation for which we are seeking. Reading can be made to sound spontaneous; officiating clergy and Readers are working from a printed text for much of the liturgy but are trying to make the words sound meaningful at every service.

Experience in reading lessons in services – no longer the sole prerogative of clergy or of Readers in the formal sense – can be a good preparation for leading intercessions. The words of scripture are fixed and given, yet they continually offer a living message, a personal challenge, and it is the business of those who read aloud to make them do so. Without making fixed assumptions, for the two activities are different, the rota of lesson readers might be seen as a possible source of intercessors. It is possible to speak fluently from memory alone, but even the most experienced preachers and lecturers usually like to have at least some written notes. There are those who can work without anything on paper, and they are to be admired, but not everyone can imitate them. In these matters, overconfidence is more dangerous than timidity.

There are many printed resources to supplement our own words, and some examples are given in Chapter 7.

Speaking the intercessions

With script or notes in hand, the intercessor comes to the point of delivery. The most sincere and polished words are not valuable unless they can be heard and understood. Pace and timing are matters on which professional actors spend a lot of time in rehearsal. Always remembering that the theatrical effect is not what is wanted in our churches, those who lead services or take any part in them should be aware of these things. There was a time when some churchpeople would speak satirically of the styles of those who differed from them. The 'High Church', as they were once known, were accused of rushing through the service and being scarcely audible, and there were indeed some who rejoiced in what they called 'the blessed murmur of the Mass'. The 'Low Church' were rebuked for going too slowly and strongly emphasising words which seemed to have only secondary meanings in their context. Now that these hostilities have abated – and where they have not it is more than time that they did – we should all be able to agree on a satisfactory mode of presentation, without losing traditions of worship which are dear to us.

Good timing requires consideration of the position and length of pauses. Silence is an important part of spoken communication – a silence which is different from the longer periods of silent waiting upon God which may strengthen our personal prayers. Intercessory prayer as practised in church services is a dialogue led by the intercessor, with cues for the congregation to add minds and voices to the petitions. The pause before the invitatory words like 'Lord, in your mercy' calls all those present to respond. The pause is not to be too long, or the people will start wondering if the leader has lost the way; not too short either, nor spoken in one breath with the closing words of the previous section, or the transition from solo to chorus of prayer will be lost.

Perfect pace and perfect timing are lost without audibility. Voice training is a specialised discipline which is not to be attempted in a few words of theory. There are books on the subject, but it will be much better if we are lucky enough to have an actor or a speech expert in the congregation who will give a little time to help others. A basic point is that audibility is not the same as loudness: shouting distorts the voice and is inappropriate in a church service. What matters most is projection – 'throwing' the voice with deliberate direction towards a distant point which is best discovered by experimenting in the building where worship will be held. The temptation to drop the voice towards the end of a sentence is strong, since it is often a mark of closure and emphasis in ordinary speech. In public, the voice needs to keep up, even rise a little, though not into an artificial lilt or the tone which suggests a question. Final consonants have to be spoken clearly and not cut off, especially at the end of long words.

Even those who have been working for some time as readers or intercessors may do well to swallow their pride and practise in the presence of others who will comment politely but honestly on clarity and audibility. Voice training sessions are exciting when they may be had, but the goal can well be reached by a little judicious experimenting in the church, heard by some who will form part of the congregation at the time of worship. There is a different resonance in a full and an empty church. Some feedback after the actual service is as important as preliminary rehearsal. If a suggestion of the theatre seems to be creeping in, let us remember that any spoken presentation to others is quite different from the spontaneity of daily conversation, and needs to be so regarded. We may well pray that our intercessions will never become a 'performance', but still not take their practical efficiency for granted.

As a final practical point, our churches often have some kind of public address system, perhaps with a 'loop' to help those with hearing difficulty. The microphone goes a long way to overcoming problems of being heard, but it needs just as much practice and testing as unaided speech. It is necessary to find the right position in relation to it, and to decide how far natural volume may need to be modified.

After all this weight of advice, consider three more encouraging thoughts:

- If the microphone suddenly sends out an excruciating noise, it is annoying and distracting, but it is the responsibility of the person in charge of the sound system, not of the intercessor.
- The people who complain most forcefully about not being able to hear seem always to choose to sit at the back, or at the place farthest from the speaker.
- Some parish clergy give the impression of taking a pride in the difficult acoustics of their church, and will tell a visiting preacher or other participant in the service that he or she will probably not be heard.

5

Dangers, Errors and Temptations

This chapter offers warnings, and advice about what not to do when leading intercessions. It may seem to read like a list of a severe teacher's comments on a piece of written work. Please be assured that the author writes from experience, with no sense of superiority, and has learned from committing these and other errors as well as listening to them. The examples given are based on reality and are not the product of a vivid and censorious imagination.

Something has already been said about spoken delivery and the use of the voice. This important physical aspect of public prayer can be trained: everyone has the potential to improve. But being heard and understood is not enough in itself. If we are not making a prepared public recitation, but are trying seriously to contribute to an act of worship, there are many other things to consider.

With the intercessions we are moving towards the end of the Ministry of the Word. The prayers are part of that ministry, and the one who leads them is working with other ministers of the service. This is not a separate personal slot; it is to be a bridge towards the Peace and the Offertory, moving into the celebration of the sacrament of Holy Communion. It is a bridge, not a barrier, and not a side-turning to lead the service temporarily into a new direction. Modern liturgical custom has taken the eucharistic intercessions away from set forms into free and individual offerings, and this has done much to release new talents into our services. But they are still part of the service, not a private performance within it. Here, as in all our Christian lives, we are to see our gifts as offerings back to God who gave them. The Bible readings prescribed for the Ministry of the Word offer a pattern for the sermon and intercessions which follow. Each Sunday suggests a theme, though not the sometimes constricting weekly headings of the *Alternative Service Book*, and seasonal and special occasions need to be honoured. More is said in the next chapter about linking readings and intercessions.

So what can go wrong, however devout the intention?

Going on too long. It may be hard to start intercessions, or any public speaking, or any piece of writing, but it can sometimes be harder to stop. This is not a matter for a stopwatch and an anxious division of sections, but the intercessions should not be out of proportion to other parts of the service. There is room for flexibility: the Bible readings are longer on some days than on others. Roughly it may be said that five minutes is a maximum. On any occasion there may be local, national or global concerns which should not be omitted. Put in simple terms of congregational response, it is better for people to be wanting a little more and given something to extend in their own prayers, than to be switching off their attention and waiting for it to stop.

Being too short. Just to be awkward, may it be suggested that it is possible to say too little instead of too much. The recital of general petitions that are not grounded in anything specific will not evoke much response from the congregation. It is a delicate balance, but we are creatures bounded by space and time in this world, and we need a focus for our intentions. The prayer of adoration that rises above these constraints is wonderful in private devotion: led intercessory prayer calls for a different approach. It is unhelpful to be too vague, and we should steer a way between unnecessary information and leaving people wondering just what they should be praying about.

Reading the news. Local information is given in the notices, pewsheet or parish magazine; wider concerns are thrust upon us daily through various media. Intercessions are not there to make these facts known to the uninformed, but to commend them to God and remind the people of the need for their prayers. Some intercessory prayers sound too much like the headlines of the current news. It may even seem as if God is being told about what is going on, in case his attention had been engaged elsewhere and some facts had not come to his notice. Fortunately, the source of our being and our hope is not a gigantic computer which might become too full to take in any more information.

Too much detail. What people need to know will, or should, have been made clear through the relevant spoken or written announcements. Our little local affairs will be as dear to God as the great global issues, and those who are responsible for them will feel strengthened by shared prayer. So let us certainly pray for meetings and social events which are part of our fellowship.

But not: 'We pray for the meeting of the PCC which will be held at 8 o'clock next Wednesday in the vestry, when the replacement of the heating system will be discussed.' God does not need to be told when and where to turn up at the meeting or to have notice of the agenda. The members will have received their papers and do not need a rallying call under cover of prayer. He and they know that 'PCC' stands for Parochial Church Council, but can we be sure that this is known to new or occasional worshippers? We do not want to leave them behind as the intercessions continue, while they wonder what is meant. 'We pray for the next meeting of the Parochial Church Council', perhaps adding prayer for whatever wisdom and grace may be especially needed.

'We pray for the people of Dystopia, a country which is at present afflicted with famine and civil war.' Today it is more difficult to avoid knowledge of global troubles than to receive it. Prayer for relief of particular suffering is proper, but is better not put in the form of statements of fact.

'We pray for Mary Bloggs who is in the County Hospital suffering from stomach trouble which needs an operation.' Our love and concern for the sick is not enhanced by clinical details, which by arousing interest or anxiety may distract from a shared response.

God who cares for the fall of a sparrow is certainly open to prayer for our minor cares as well as the greater issues. In private prayer there is no limit to what we may bring before him, provided it is not simply selfish or for the harm of others. The comfort which comes from asking, and thus putting our worries into words, is itself a gift of divine grace. Public prayer needs to be no less directed, but to be more economical. Sometimes precision can become ludicrous and suggests a refusal of personal responsibility. Praying that the overhead projector will work at the next discussion group – an actual example – takes away from the serious concern for the overall result of the occasion. It is good to pray that the vicar's family may have a refreshing holiday, without enumerating all their travel details.

Breach of confidence. The case of Mary Bloggs brings us to another matter. Too much particularity can trespass on confidentiality. Clergy, doctors, lawyers and all whose professions bring them close to the lives of other people have to develop a habit of total confidentiality. Those who preach, or who lead public prayer, should see themselves under the same obligation, whatever their work outside the church may be. Be wary of personal details given about other people. There is malicious gossip, which is obvious and should be easy to avoid, and there is gossip which is intended to be harmless but can be damaging even if the facts in question are true and not sensational. There are people whose idea of something confidential is 'only to be told to one person at a time'. Christian communities seem to be particularly prone to excessive interest in the lives of others – perhaps a dark twist of temptation in the proper duty of care and concern. How often is something whispered as 'not to be repeated – just telling you for prayer'.

So be sure not to reveal personal or embarrassing information through the prayers, however good the intention may be. The official public list in the magazine or pewsheet should be a safe guide, but an extra check may be advisable. If in any doubt, have a quiet word with the priest or minister, or with the parish pastoral group, or even speak to the people concerned. Do not rely on their friends, who may be full of sympathy but unsure about what is expected. Mary Bloggs may welcome prayer but not want all her details to be known. Some people do not like even the basic knowledge of their troubles to be mentioned in church. Some object quite strongly to a yearly commemoration by name of their own dead relatives while others appreciate and are comforted by it.

Disagreements and disputes, between groups or individuals, can be offered for reconciliation in private prayer, but not in public intercessions. Well-meaning attempts at making peace by making known are likely to stir up more trouble. Christians are as liable as others to fall out among themselves, and are not free from the temptation to find some pleasure in knowing a little more about problems in the community. It is nothing new: St Paul had trouble with two pious women in the church at Philippi:

> I urge Euodias and I urge Syntyche to be of the same mind in the Lord.
> Philippians 4.2

Inadvertent offence. Be careful with lists of names. Whether they be offered for healing, support or simply in love and gratitude, it is better to mention none than to omit one. This is a particular danger when making a speech of thanks to a number of people, but it can creep into intercessions as well. When you pray, as we should, for local clergy and Readers, or for those to be married or baptised, either make sure that the list is complete or make a more general petition. Also, check that the right needs or duties are being attached to the right people.

Personal prejudices. Those who volunteer to lead intercessions – or agree to be volunteered into the job – are not likely consciously to use the opportunity for their own advantage. But we all have our own preferences and prejudices, and indeed our individual diversity is part of the glory of God's creation. Christian values should inform and support Christian intercessions, but there is no place for being judgemental. This is not the time for asking for changes in what we happen to disapprove. Prayer for the repeal of a piece of public legislation which the intercessor did not like has been heard in a service, and resulted later in a bitter dispute which marred what had gone before. Nor are we loudly to lament the state of public morality, or to pray that authority will be harder – or softer – in specific directions. There is a temptation, which probably no one quite escapes, of being one of those who as Samuel Butler says,

> Compound for sins they are inclined to
> By damning those they have no mind to.

Unnecessary emphasis. There are some words much loved by those who pray in public which do not add anything to sincere petitions. 'We *just* pray' suggests that we might be asking a lot more but are being restrained. 'We *really* pray' sounds as if we are now coming to a point of importance which somehow had been lacking before. 'We *do* pray' – make no mistake about it, that is actually what we are doing. Let us all listen for favourite and often repeated words which are not doing any useful work, and try to manage without them. This is a matter where we may need to summon up our humility and ask someone to point out such verbal mannerisms.

It is indeed with humility that this didactic chapter is offered, and with deep desire than no one will be frightened away from the intercessor's task. No one will become completely free from all errors, and the God to whom we pray looks with love on our true intentions. All we can do is to respond with our best to the positive sense of a great privilege, the work of divine mercy in which we are allowed to share.

6

Preparing for the Service

Whatever we learn about general principles of intercessory prayer, and the techniques of its presentation, the time comes when the person charged with intercessions on a particular Sunday or other occasion has to prepare to stand up and speak. The conscientious intercessor will not leave it until the evening before the service, but will be thinking about it during the week.

Prayerful preparation

The first approach to preparation is prayer, the call which the Christian hears and answers before beginning any serious task. This is prayer about prayer, a special petition for help and guidance brought into our regular prayers when the duty of intercessions comes round. Preparation to lead intercessions will be part of the preparation for communion which every communicant should practise. The fact that the Eucharist has become the main Sunday service in most churches is a cause for great thanksgiving, but there is a danger that regular attendance can begin to erode the sense of reverence with which the sacrament should be approached. Its grace is free and absolute, but not to be taken lightly. Those who help to lead the service, whether clergy or laity, need specially careful and prayerful preparation. Many like to make a special intention for the day, and grace for the work would be an appropriate intention of the one who is to intercede.

Bible-based intercessions

Study the readings appointed for the day. They may be printed in advance on the weekly pewsheet, but anyone who joins the list of intercessors should have the lectionary for the year. Give careful consideration to how they relate to one another and use them to find some themes for the day. Without going into advanced Bible study, a commentary may help to bring out ideas, but a sincere personal approach is better than simply following another's opinion, however scholarly. The Gospel is particularly important and may offer the principal inspiration. The lectionary now used in most churches provides for the continuous reading of one of the Synoptic Gospels – Matthew, Mark and Luke – for most Sundays through the year and thus encourages a sequence of reflections on the life of our Lord. Many published outlines for intercessions are based on the appointed readings.

The seasons of the Church's year will of course influence the general tone of the intercessions. The joyful note of Christmas and Easter, the solemn reflections of Advent, the penitence of Lent, are felt all through the service and are picked up when the time comes for united prayer. It is more difficult to find the right note for the long season from Trinity to Advent, and the shorter period between the Presentation and Ash Wednesday, both sometimes known rather discouragingly as Ordinary Time. Too often the conclusion of the cycle which follows the life of our Lord from his Nativity to his Ascension and the descent of the Holy Spirit brings a certain slackness in both private and public devotion, a feeling that there is nothing in particular to concentrate our prayers. These are the weeks in which all that has been learned and meditated upon should be feeding our worship. Pentecost is sometimes called 'the birthday of the Church', and a birthday is not an end but a beginning. This is when the Church still seeks to do the work of God in this world, through faithful obedience in daily life, in the routine of work and recreation, relationship with family and strangers, upheld by the times of shared worship and private prayer. The readings for each Sunday and festival provide plenty of ideas, and life around us goes on as vividly as it does in the more exciting ecclesiastical times.

When the more obvious themes of a season are not presenting themselves, ideas and images in the Bible may help our prayers, give them some colour and prevent them from becoming too abstract. Both the Old and the New Testaments have shaped our Christian thinking and given specific ways of expressing the ultimately inexpressible nature and work of God. These images of the Bible are continually inspiring, but need to be used with some caution. There are what might be called first-order images, such as the Sonship of Christ, which constantly support our praying and writing about the faith. Others, second-order images, are traditional and beautiful but not always so directly communicative to a present-day congregation. Many will indeed respond with instant devotion to ideas of the shepherd and his flock, of vineyards and fishing, but we have to be always thinking not only of regular worshippers but also of occasional visitors who may not know their Bible so well. The readings for the day may have put such pictures into an understandable context which will bring them naturally into the intercessions, but beware of the fallen sparrow or barren fig tree which may try to creep in, without being so significant to everyone as to the intercessor.

Being cautious but wisely imaginative with such details, we remember again that the intercessions are an integral part of the whole service and should be clearly related to what has gone before. It may be helpful to consult with the preacher and pick up some references from the sermon. This may encourage your priest or minister to think about preparing the sermon well in advance!

Current issues

The message of the Bible will be our chief guide, but we need also to be firmly rooted in the needs of the present. It is good to be well acquainted with what is going on in the locality, and especially around regular members of the congregation, while being wary of the dangers of gossip, conjecture and breach of confidentiality which have already been mentioned. Such local and domestic matters help to give relevance to this part of the service. The need to be continually 'relevant' is a present-day anxiety which sometimes causes the playing down of eternal truths and unwelcome obligations, but it is a proper concern in planning and conducting services. As well as the weekly church pewsheet, the diocesan or circuit notes will probably offer particular parishes, organisations or overseas links to be remembered in the prayers.

We are to pray also for the world, not as something separated from the holy, but as needing to be infused by the beauty of holiness to restore all that is wrong in its present state. It is a good world, the world of God's creation and continual concern, grievously damaged but not destroyed. If we are to pray intelligently for the world beyond our own locality, we need to be well informed about it. Our shared humanity has never been more apparent than at this time of shrinking distances, fragile frontiers and economic interdependence summed up in the ugly but necessary word 'globalisation'. Awareness of the world should strengthen our desire to offer in prayer the concern which cannot always be expressed in practical help. In fact, we can hardly fail to be aware of what is going on, since information is continually poured out in print and sound and vision. There is much cause for sorrow and sympathy to be given words in our intercessions. There is also much for which to give thanks, and our prayers can be for the furtherance of good endeavours as well as for the relief of suffering. The media give us a disproportionate amount of the bad news.

Once again, be precise and focused, but do not make the prayers heavy with too much detail. There is no need to inform God or the congregation about exactly what is happening, but careful thought will make what is said more meaningful and draw out a stronger response from the listeners. Knowledge of current affairs and intelligent application are no substitute for Holy Wisdom, but wisdom does not leave knowledge and intelligence at the church door.

Using published material

Will you rely entirely on your own composition, or will you use one or more of the printed resources available? Some examples of these will be given in the next chapter; they are generally not intended to be read out in full, but leave spaces for specific names and causes to be inserted. Do not feel constrained by printed forms – they are meant to help, not to inhibit. Do more than just inserting a few names, and feel free to expand what has already been written. There is no need to try to conform entirely to the style of the source book. Style is an individual thing and seems false if it is deliberately imitated. However, the style may be helpful as a guide and do something to shape additional material into words.

There is no lack of fine prayers in the Christian tradition, though not many of them are directly intercessory. But there are resources here which may be used as a closure to the intercessions, or perhaps at the end of a section. It may be necessary to revise traditional language to make it fit the rest of the intercessions. This is something already considered. Immediacy and shared understanding are essential in church intercessions, but traditional prayers can add solemnity and recollection that we are praying with the whole Church not only now but throughout all ages. Our forerunners in the faith can sometimes protect us in prayer against triviality or a cult of the self.

Congregational response

The intercessor leads the prayer, but there is another party to the intercessions – the congregation – and they too need preparation. The whole Church prays together every time the Eucharist is celebrated. In this part of the Ministry of the Word, we are offering the prayers of the faithful, concentrated in a particular part of the Holy, Catholic and Apostolic Church, a small part perhaps but no less precious to God than parts that are bigger and outwardly more impressive. It is not selfish or presumptuous to put all our devotion for the moment into what is immediate. The intercessory prayer in the Book of Common Prayer expresses it:

> To all thy people give thy heavenly grace, and especially to this congregation here present.

The members of the congregation here present should be more than passive listeners.

This is where the lay intercessor will need to turn to the priest or minister with overall responsibility for the services. A sermon on the place and importance of the intercessions in the service will arouse any in the congregation who are in the habit of going off into their own thoughts when the intercessions begin. A short piece in the weekly pewsheet or the parish magazine could support the spoken word and give people time for reflection. The power of our joint prayers would be strengthened if more of the regular worshippers followed the advice given to intercessors, to inform themselves about global and local needs, to add these to their own prayers, and to pray for those who lead intercessions on their behalf. Perhaps the clergy or experienced lay people could lead a workshop for intercessors in an evening or weekend.

The intercessions offer a time in the service when the rest of the congregation can put down their prayer books or service sheets, just listen and respond. We have become a generation more centred on the text or the screen than on the spoken word. Worshippers often have their noses in the printed words of the service which should have become familiar by weekly use. The readings for the day are often printed and are followed by the eye even while the reader is bringing them to the ear. The intercessions bring a splendid opportunity to concentrate on the spoken words and let them guide our thoughts and commitment. Liturgy is essentially something to be spoken and it is a loss that today the oral tradition has given way to the textual.

When there is a committed listening congregation, it is back to the intercessor, guided by the Holy Spirit, to make the prayers meaningful to them. If all are drawn to what is being offered in prayer, intercessor and congregation working together, there will be a powerful force for good. It is in these united prayers where all motives of selfishness and convenience are swept aside, that the little local congregation may know itself to be part of the great universal Church and be made ready for the supreme prayer of all, the eucharistic prayer. The closing words of the intercessions, said by the intercessor or the presiding minister, conclude the Ministry of the Word and open the way to the celebration of the holy sacrament.

7

Examples and Opinions

Here are a few examples of published outlines for intercessions related to a particular Sunday or other celebration, followed by a commentary on their connection with the appointed Bible readings and the theme for the day. The breaks between the sentences suggest places for the addition of particular names, or for local or topical concerns. The first three are based on the Gospel for the day.

SECOND SUNDAY OF ADVENT YEAR B

Mark 1.1–8

In the confidence of the Gospel, let us pray to the Lord.

Let the Church give thanks and praise for the good news of salvation, and receive the power to proclaim it to the world . . . May all Christian people prepare in humility and love to celebrate the coming of Christ.

Grant to the whole world the knowledge of the divine mercy revealed in Jesus Christ, that all people may come through repentance to new life . . . Make straight the crooked ways of the world and give light to the dark places.

Give us grace to be messengers of the good news to those

whose lives come near to our own . . . Send the healing power of the Holy Spirit to guide all in our community into the way of peace.

Have mercy on all who are held in the power of unrepented sin, and lead them back into the right way . . . Strengthen those who suffer indifference and hostility as they preach the word of God.

We give thanks for those who in this world received the word of salvation, showed its power in their lives and are now at rest . . . Keep us faithful in the way where they have gone before, until we come to the Kingdom.

May our prayers be accepted through Christ by whom we are baptised in the Holy Spirit.

Commentary

This Sunday is associated in the Advent sequence with John the Baptist. It does not celebrate his birth or martyrdom, but his role as the forerunner of our Lord. John is seen as the last of the Prophets of the Old Covenant and the first herald of the New. The Advent themes of expectation and repentance are emphasised. The first verse proclaims 'the good news of Jesus Christ, the Son of God'. 'Good news' translates the Greek *evangelion* – 'gospel' in the King James Version, probably the first use of the word in this specifically Christian sense. It is therefore appropriate to give prominence to the Gospel in the opening call to prayer and the prayer for the Church, before calling all believers to remember the Advent message.

The Gospel is not only for committed Christians, but for all humanity. The prayer picks up the quotation from Isaiah, originally a message of hope to the Israelites in exile. The proclamation is not only for authorised clergy and preachers but a message of hope which each of us should be telling wherever we can. Then the prayer for the suffering is especially for those who cannot find the way to freedom from their sins, and for those who, like the Baptist, suffer for telling the good news. Advent also reminds us of the final judgement and the life to come, and our fellowship with the faithful departed.

The Gospel reading ends with John's announcement of Jesus, the greater One who will baptise with the Holy Spirit, and the intercessions are offered in the assurance of the grace of our own baptism.

THE EPIPHANY

Matthew 2.1–12

Let us kneel in homage as we pray to God, the King of Kings.

We offer our richest gifts of prayer and praise, knowing them imperfect but trusting in the holiness of Christ to make them holy ... As the Wise Men were led by a star to Bethlehem, so guide your pilgrim Church to worship in holiness and bow down in adoration until the time when your purpose is accomplished.

Give wisdom to the rulers of this world, that they may see the light of truth and follow the way of peace ... Let them not be moved by fear or envy; make them ready to see you in what seems small and unimportant, so that their power is used not in pride but in service.

As we have known the joy of Christmas and rejoiced in the gift of the Holy Child, may we now bring to him our gifts of love and reverence ... Make our lives, in our families and in all our meeting with others, tokens of the treasures that in our hearts we offer to the Lord.

Look with mercy on those whose journeys through the world are long and can see no guiding star . . . Bring them through the hard places of sickness and sorrow until they may set down their burdens and rest . . . Give grace to those who are seeking truth and cannot find their way: lead them to the feet of Christ.

Receive the souls of the departed into the kingdom where all journeys end and all worship is fulfilled in glory . . . As little Bethlehem was made great by the divine birth, so may those who were humble and unregarded in this world be numbered with the saints in heaven.

We make our offering of prayer through Christ, King, Priest and atoning Sacrifice.

Commentary

The visit of the Magi to Bethlehem is so often read as part of the Christmas story that the Epiphany may be neglected as a great festival in its own right. It commemorates the first revelation of the incarnate Christ to the Gentile world, and introduces a season of Sunday readings which in various ways tell of further revelations of his glory. 'Epiphany' means a showing forth, and it is not just the end of the twelve days of Christmas but the beginning of what the Nativity meant to the whole world. The theme is worship and offering, picked up in the opening sentence and then emphasised as the continuing duty of the Church, both collectively and for each of its individual members.

A later tradition made the Magi into kings, and although it

has no Gospel support there is a lesson of humility and wisdom here for all who hold power, and we pray for them.

The congregation will still be in the Christmas mood, though perhaps a little jaded and feeling that it is all over for another year. Let our prayers remind them that what they have celebrated is not an end but a beginning, and that we all have gifts to offer to the Christ Child through our service of others.

The Magi had a long, hard journey, and God who guided them will guide those who trust in him in every age through the difficulties of life's journey. The journey must end for all in death and new life, where the distinctions of this world will pass away.

The closing words remind us of the traditional meaning attached to the gifts of gold, frankincense and myrrh.

PROPER 13 (NINTH SUNDAY AFTER TRINITY) YEAR C

Luke 12.13–21

Let us pray for the Church and for the world, that in all things they may be rich towards God.

Shield the Church from temptation to seek the wealth and power that pass away . . . Bless her with the true wealth which makes her a faithful servant, eager to fulfil his word.

We pray for the rich of the world, that they shall be spared from the dangers of pride and moved to use their wealth for the general good . . . Grant wisdom and justice to those who must make decisions in conflicting interests.

When we are at ease with our families and friends, let us never forget that all we enjoy is a gift from above . . . Help us to be thankful for what we possess, free from greed for what we do not have, and generous in what we are able to give.

Bring relief to the poor who have suffered from the greed of the rich, as individuals or as whole nations . . . Have mercy on those who have been overcome by foolish greed and brought to ruin.

We pray for all who have died suddenly and unprepared . . . May the abundant mercy of divine love receive them into life . . . Teach us to live as souls that are ready for the call of God.

We pray in the name of Christ, our only hope and assurance.

Commentary

The Gospel for today contains some of the teaching of Jesus about the right attitude towards money and possessions. He refuses to arbitrate in a dispute about an inheritance, warns his hearers to remember that covetousness is a sin and that the meaning of life does not lie in how much we own, and then tells the parable of the rich man who thought complacently that his wealth would continue to increase but died suddenly. Our prayers are directed towards following these warnings for ourselves and remembering our duty in the proper use of money.

The Church needs to be continually watchful against the temptation of worldly power and success, and to seek the spiritual treasure which does not fade away.

The world today is dominated by finance to a degree which can be harmful to the integrity of the very rich and cause difficulties in the best allocation of resources. We in our less influential lives still need to be good stewards of what has been entrusted to us and to act responsibly in our situation.

These thoughts draw us towards intercession for those to whom money has meant suffering, either by lack of necessities or by misuse of wealth. Many are being ruined today by the temptations of easy borrowing, gambling or bad speculation.

The parable of the 'Rich Fool' prompts us to pray for all who are similarly taken by sudden death and for recognition of our own mortality. All is offered in the faith that we shall find strength in Christ to follow his commands.

(Intercession from Raymond Chapman, *Hear Our Prayer*, London: Canterbury Press, 2003)

The next intercessions draw on the Gospel and the other readings appointed for the occasion.

CONVERSION OF ST PAUL

Acts 9.11–22
Matthew 19.27–end

Called to be followers of Christ, let us pray for his Church and for his world.

As Paul was appointed for the increase of the Church at its beginning, so may the Church in our day grow in faith and wisdom and be true to the Gospel which he preached . . . We give thanks for those who have gone out into many lands to spread the word of the Lord and we pray for missionaries and teachers of the faith . . . We pray that all who confess the faith of Christ may be united in love for him and for one another.

Give peace among the nations, that their diverse ways may be brought into harmony for the good of all humanity . . . Teach the powerful to learn the wisdom of simplicity and the strength of gentleness.

As Paul found friends to shelter and sustain him in his journeying, make us more ready to receive the stranger and the wanderer in the love of God . . . Make our homes holy and prayerful, remembering the houses where the first believers met for worship.

We pray for all who suffer for their faith . . . As Saul the persecutor became Paul the Apostle, let the eyes of those who hate God's people be opened to the truth . . . We pray too for all who travel, those in perilous places, and those who are weary with long wandering.

Grant that those who have come to the end of their journey here on earth may find rest and peace at the last . . . Bring them into the company of blessed Paul and of all the saints who have fought the good fight and stood firm to the end.

We pray in the name of Jesus Christ who chose Paul for his own and empowered him to preach with holy wisdom.

Commentary

Commemoration of the saints has been practised by the Church since its early years, and we are now more often observing the principal feasts in our Calendar. The readings for each saint will give a focus for the intercessions. They all answered the call to holiness but each was called as an individual with a special place in the divine purpose. St Paul was called from being a persecutor to become a missionary to the Gentile world as well as to the Jews.

We remember how the Church in our time still has the duty to preach the Gospel, and how some have followed the calling of St Paul to devote their lives to its service. There is also a reminder that the feast has been taken as the close of the Week of Christian Unity.

As Paul changed from being a savage persecutor to being a messenger of love, we pray for a change of heart in the world and its leaders, still troubled by strife and controversy like the world which he knew.

The New Testament story of Paul's missionary journeys tells of the many friends who helped him and received him into their homes, and we pray that we may follow their example. It tells also of much suffering and hardship, and we know that there are many who do not have our security and the freedom to proclaim and practise the faith.

Our life here on earth is like a journey in which we meet both joys and sorrows. We try to follow it with the courage of Paul and his companions, and be led to its heavenly goal.

Paul put his trust in Christ alone and we pray in the same confidence.

There are other services, not in the traditional Calendar, which have become a regular and loved part of yearly worship. The Harvest Thanksgiving stands for a timeless human instinct to rejoice in the harvest. As an act of united Christian worship it seems to have been started in 1843 by a Cornish priest, R. S. Hawker. The Bible offers many relevant readings, and the prayers which follow are based on the general theme rather than specific passages.

HARVEST THANKSGIVING

Let us pray to God, the Lord of the harvest in all things material and spiritual.

As you have blessed the Church with abundant grace, keep her faithful in the offering of word and sacrament, knowing that all things come from you and return to you . . . Send out your labourers to gather the harvest of the world, that all may know the riches of your love.

We pray for all who work that others may be fed, for those who bring in the harvest of the land and the sea . . . We pray for those employed in the processing and transport of food . . . Grant a more just distribution of the goods of the world.

Give to us, our families and friends, grateful hearts for all your bounty and a concern for the needs of others . . . Bless those who work to bring meals to the poor and infirm in this community.

We pray for all who are hungry and undernourished . . . We pray especially for the children whose health is damaged by lack of food . . . Bless those who work for the relief of famine.

We give thanks for the departed who have been gathered into your care . . . Grant them the joy of faith brought to fruition in your heavenly kingdom.

We offer our prayers, desiring to be faithful labourers for the harvest of Christ's kingdom.

Commentary

This a time to praise God for all his bounty and to start with thanksgiving for his loving control of every aspect of life. This thought is carried into the prayer for the Church, his steward and messenger on earth, with a reminder of the words of Jesus to his disciples:

'Look around you, and see how the fields are ripe for harvesting.'
John 4.35

In this service it is appropriate to remember how food is essential to human life and to remember the ethical implications of sharing for all people. This leads us to offer our gratitude for what we too often take for granted and to bring universal needs nearer to home.

The suffering most in our minds at this time will be the hunger and the actual starvation in many countries, arousing our resolve to help in some way the work of relief.

Jesus also used the image of harvest to speak of the Last Judgement (Matthew 13.24–30), and we can think of the dead as those whose harvest he has brought home.

These thoughts of mission, care for others and perseverance in the faith are gathered together in the final offering.

(Intercession from Raymond Chapman, *Leading Intercessions*, London: Canterbury Press, enlarged edition, 2006)

Finally, some thoughts about intercessory prayer, gathered from writers across several centuries.

I urge that supplications, prayers, intercessions, and thanksgivings should be made for everyone, for kings and all who are in high positions, so that we may lead a quiet and peaceable life in all godliness and dignity.
1 Timothy 2.1

St Paul, writing to Timothy, exhorteth him to make *prayers and supplications for all men*, exempting none, of what degree or state soever they be. In which place he maketh mention by name of *kings and rulers, which are in authority*, putting us thereby to knowledge, how greatly it concerneth the profit of the commonwealth, to pray diligently for the higher powers. Neither is it without good cause, that he doth so often, in all his Epistles crave the prayers of God's people for himself. For in so doing, he declareth to the world, how expedient and needful it is, daily to call upon God, for the ministers of his holy word and sacraments, that they *may have the door of utterance opened* unto them, that they may truly understand the Scriptures, that they may effectually preach the same unto the people, and bring forth the true fruits thereof, to the example of all other. After this sort did the congregation continually pray for Peter at Jerusalem, and for Paul among the Gentiles, to the great increase and furtherance of Christ's Gospel. And if we, following their good example herein, will study to do the like, doubtless it cannot be expressed, how greatly we shall both help ourselves, and also please God.

Second Book of Homilies, 1562, 'Concerning Prayer'

Of prayer there are two uses. It serveth as a mean to procure those things which God hath promised to grant when we ask; and it serveth as a mean to express our lawful desires also towards that, which whether we shall have or no, we know not, till we see the event. Things in themselves unholy or unseemly, we may not ask; we may whatsoever, being not forbidden, either Nature or Grace shall reasonably move us to wish as importing the good of men; albeit God himself have nowhere by promise assured us of that particular which our prayer craveth. To pray for that which is in itself, and of its own nature, apparently a thing impossible, were not convenient. Wherefore, though men do without offence wish daily that the affairs which with evil success are past, might have fallen out much better; yet to pray that they may have been any other than they are, this being a manifest impossibility in itself, the rules of Religion do not permit. Whereas contrariwise, when things of their own nature contingent and mutable, are by the secret determination of

God appointed one way, though we the other way make our prayers, and consequently ask those things of God, which are by this supposition impossible, we notwithstanding do not hereby in prayer transgress our lawful bounds.

Richard Hooker, *Laws of Ecclesiastical Polity*, 1594

Almighty and everliving God, who by thy holy Apostle hast taught us to make prayers and supplications, and to give thanks, for all men: We humbly beseech thee most mercifully [*to accept our alms and oblations, and] to receive these our prayers, which we offer unto thy Divine Majesty; beseeching thee to inspire continually the universal Church with the spirit of truth, unity, and concord: And grant, that all they that do confess thy holy Name may agree in the truth of thy holy Word, and live in unity, and godly love. We beseech thee also to save and defend all Christian Kings, Princes, and Governors; and specially thy servant ELIZABETH our Queen; that under her we may be godly and quietly governed: And grant unto her whole Council, and to all that are put in authority under her, that they may truly and indifferently minister justice, to the punishment of wickedness and vice, and to the maintenance of thy true religion, and virtue. Give grace, O heavenly Father, to all Bishops and Curates, that they may both by their life and doctrine set forth thy true and lively Word, and rightly and duly administer thy holy Sacraments: And to all thy people give thy heavenly grace; and specially to this congregation here present; that, with meek heart and due reverence, they may hear, and receive thy holy Word; truly serving thee in holiness and righteousness all the days of their life. And we most humbly beseech thee of thy goodness, O Lord, to comfort and succour all them, who in this transitory life are in trouble, sorrow, need, sickness, or any other adversity. And we also bless thy holy Name for all thy servants departed this life in thy faith and fear; beseeching thee to give us grace so to follow their good examples, that with them we may be partakers of thy heavenly kingdom: Grant this, O Father, for Jesus Christ's sake, our only Mediator and Advocate. Amen.

If there be no alms or oblations, then shall the words [of accepting our alms and oblations] *be left out unsaid.*

Prayer for the Church Militant, Book of Common Prayer, 1662

The first followers of Christ seem to support all their love, and to maintain all their intercourse and correspondence, by mutual prayers for one another.

St. Paul, whether he writes to churches or particular persons, shows his intercession to be perpetual for them, that they are the constant subject of his prayers.

Thus to the Philippians, 'I thank my God upon every remembrance of you, always in every prayer of mine for you all making request with joy.' Here we see, not only a continual intercession, but performed with so much gladness, as shows that it was an exercise of love in which he highly rejoiced . . .

Apostles and great saints did not only thus benefit and bless particular churches, and private persons; but they themselves also received graces from God by the prayers of others. Thus saith St. Paul to the Corinthians: 'You also help together by prayer for us, that for the gift bestowed upon us by the means of many persons thanks may be given by many on our behalf.'

This was the ancient friendship of Christians, uniting and cementing their hearts, not by worldly considerations, or human passions, but by the mutual communication of spiritual blessings, by prayers and thanksgivings to God for one another.

It was his holy intercession that raised Christians to such a state of mutual love, as far exceeded all that had been praised and admired in human friendship. And when the same spirit of intercession is again in the world, when Christianity has the same power over the hearts of people that it then had, this holy friendship will be in fashion, and Christians will be again the wonder of the world, for that exceeding love which they bear to one another.

For a frequent intercession with God, earnestly beseeching Him to forgive the sins of all mankind, to bless them with His providence, enlighten them with His Spirit, and bring them to everlasting happiness, is the divinest exercise that the heart of man can be engaged in.

William Law, *A Serious Call to a Devout and Holy Life*, 1728, London: Epworth Press, 1961

This is the force of prayer, that it is a calling down of God into ourselves, a going forth of ourselves to God. A calling of God into ourselves, for our Blessed Lord says, 'Shall not your Heavenly Father give the Holy Spirit to them that ask Him?' a going forth of ourselves to God, for the Spirit which He hath given us, 'maketh intercession for us'. It is not we alone who pray, if we pray aright; but He, our Lord, Who is prayed by us, Himself prayeth in us, by His Holy Spirit which He hath given us. Our prayers go up unto the Throne of God, because they are His Voice in us.

E. B. Pusey, *Parochial and Cathedral Sermons*, Oxford: Parker, 1882

You might, on Rogation days, I think, ask God to send rain. They say all the country wants rain, and it seems to be delayed. Well, why not ask God to send rain, gracious rain, on His inheritance, and to refresh it? What good will that do? Well, your prayer would lie inside the eternal predestination and providence of God, and belong to that power which ordereth all things in heaven and earth, because it not only ordereth all things concerning the rain, but it ordereth your prayer. That is when the prayer is powerful; it lieth within the eternal foreknowledge, like your life and destiny, within the eternal providence and foreknowledge of God.

A. H. Stanton, *Father Stanton's Last Sermons*, London: Hodder & Stoughton, 1914

In intercession as a whole we have the simplest example provided by the general religious life, of a vast principle which is yet largely unexplored by us. It is the principle, that man's emergent will and energy can join itself to, and work with, the supernatural forces for the accomplishment of the work of God: sometimes for this purpose even entering into successful conflict with the energies of the 'natural world'.

Evelyn Underhill, *Man and the Supernatural*, London: Methuen, 1934

Perhaps one of the joys reserved for us hereafter will be to learn what became of our intercessions, and to meet the souls they supported in time of need. And for ourselves, there will be the joy of meeting those who have prayed for us, and so of realising from a new angle our share in the Communion of Saints. If so, we may learn then how much the Church owes, and we ourselves as members of it, to the artless prayers uttered by simple child-like souls, the value of whose intercession we should have little suspected.

Herbert Northcott, *The Venture of Prayer*, London: SPCK, 1962

Some people are dismayed by the thought of the number of people and causes who should have a place in their prayers. The great host of those for whom they have failed to find room in their devout attention stretches out into the imagined distance, each one an accusation. This is an unnecessary perplexity which disperses as we see our intercessions as our participation in the saving action of the Body of Christ. Obviously we cannot embrace the whole world in our thought; but God can. If our prayer is part of the intercession of the great High Priest, whose love spans the universe, we can play our part in it with gladness and seriousness and without agitation. It is clearly God's will that we bring into our prayers those whose lives he has closely interlocked with ours in the three worlds which constitute most of our life, the worlds of our family, our friendships and our work. We shall also join in the wider intercessions of the liturgical life of the Church.

J. Neville Ward, *The Use of Praying*, London: Epworth Press, 1967

Serious intercession always seeks to express itself in personal and specific terms. Are these ideas there just to be overruled or ignored, if they do not coincide with God's wiser knowledge of what is 'Best'? This is how many people think of the matter, but to do so is to relapse once more into an external and impersonal conception. These particular requests of ours spring from the common life we share with those for whom we pray; they are the concrete articulation at the conscious level of the unseen but real bond that unites us. Because that bond is a living one of mutual influence, they do not merely state the possibilities to which we suppose the other person might be open. They help to create an openness for these things. When, therefore, through this natural medium of our psychical communion the love of God is brought to bear on the other person, its power works within the existing potentials, and thus issues in those very changes (or ones akin to them) for which we have asked. In this way human freedom is respected, human co-operation with God is made real, and yet prayer is genuinely answered.

John Austin Baker, *The Foolishness of God*, London: Darton, Longman and Todd, 1970

The God of Christian prayer is an involved God, a social God. Involvement and society are among the essential marks of Christian prayer because this prayer is actually a participation in God. God is involved in humanity, and so prayer is an involvement in humanity. God is social and not isolated, and so prayer is a social, not an isolated, activity. There is a fundamental solidarity about prayer which is central to the Christian understanding. The taking of manhood into God embraces spirituality and politics, the inner and outer worlds, in one process.

Kenneth Leech, *True Prayer*, London: SPCK, 1980

People who are invited to lead the prayers of others are called upon to speak not just for themselves but for all creation and even for God himself. In the service of Holy Communion they are required to express and invoke the grace of God at the feast of the Kingdom of Heaven. Since nobody can do these things adequately, nobody need be ashamed to try. If they acknowledge their inability the Holy Spirit will direct their hearts and minds as they prepare the words they propose to speak.

R. Hockley, *Intercessions at Holy Communion*, London: Mowbray, 1981

The Prayers of the Church are the voice of the Messianic people. This is a corporate voice in which everything that is human finds utterance, in such a way that one speaks with the voice of all, and all speak with the voice of each one. No prayer (not even the most public or ceremonious) is ever anything but personal, for prayer implies by definition a movement of the heart towards God. It has been said that 'Liturgical forms which are authentic are born from the personal prayer of an individual with his Creator and then fixed in forms suited to communal expression. The Psalter is the most typical example of this.' This means that the Church's prayer, by catching up each and every human experience and offering it for cleansing, healing and reconciling, or for thanksgiving and praising, or for dedication and sacrifice and service, is affirming the eternal value and significance of all that happens within the human life that has been experienced also by the Son of God.

George Appleton, *The Oxford Book of Prayer*, Oxford: OUP, 1988

Intercession is a way in which we share with Jesus in bearing God's anger at the sin and evil in the world, so that like Moses we stand in the breach on behalf of the world (cf. Psalm 106.23). It is a way in which we share God's anguish over the world and it is a way in which we enter the fight against the evil powers.

John Gaden, *A Vision of Wholeness*, Harrisburg: Morehouse, 1995

When praying do not give God instructions – report for duty.

Anonymous, source unknown

A Prayer for the Intercessor

Lord, speak through my lips, to ask on behalf of the congregation those things which are needful for them and pleasing in your sight. Make me fluent in speech but not loving my own invention, brief in words but not abrupt in utterance. Make me an instrument of the worship which we offer together. I ask for this grace through Jesus Christ, our eternal Mediator and Intercessor.

Further Resources

Raymond Chapman, *Hear Our Prayer*, London: Canterbury Press, 2003
> Prayers for every Sunday in Years A, B and C, and for some special occasions, based on the Gospel for the day in the Revised Common Lectionary.

Raymond Chapman, *Leading Intercessions*, London: Canterbury Press, enlarged edition, 2006
> Prayers for every Sunday in Years A, B and C, for all the major holy days, for baptisms, weddings, funerals, and other special services, based on the Scripture readings for the day in the Revised Common Lectionary.

Christine Odell, *Companion to the Revised Common Lectionary, Volume 1: Intercessions*, London: Epworth, 1998
John Pritchard, *The Intercessions Handbook*, London: SPCK, 1997
John Pritchard, *The Second Intercessions Handbook*, London: SPCK, 2004
> Prayers through the year based on the readings for services using the Revised Common Lectionary.

W. C. Collins, *Intercessions at the Parish Communion*, London: Mowbray, 1985

> Designed for use with the themes of the discontinued *Alternative Service Book*, but still suitable for many Sundays through the year.

R. Hockley, *Intercessions at Holy Communion*, London: Mowbray, 1981

> Also designed for use with the *Alternative Service Book*, covering the seasons of the Church year and with some useful suggestions for particular needs and topics.

Dorothy McRae-McMahon, *Liturgies for High Days*, London: SPCK, 2006

Times and Seasons, London: Church House Publishing, 2006

> Two books of resources to supplement the set liturgies, including some suggestions for intercessions.

George Appleton (ed.), *The Oxford Book of Prayer*, Oxford: OUP, 1988

Mary Bachelor (ed.), *The Lion Prayer Collection*, Oxford: Lion Publishing, 1993

The SPCK Book of Christian Prayer, London: SPCK, 1995

> Collections with a wide range of traditional and modern prayers, including some suitable to use or adapt in intercessions.

Name and Subject Index

Scripture References Index